THE
I
CHING
WORKBOOK

R. L. WING

HARMONY
BOOKS · NEW YORK

ACKNOWLEDGMENTS

The author is grateful to many contributors to this book.
They know who they are. Special thanks to Martin Inn for his sensitive editing
and to Fred Cline of the Asian Art Library in San Francisco
for his generous assistance.

Published in the United State by Harmony Books, an imprint of the Crown
Publishing Group, a division of Penguin Random House LLC, New York.

Harmony Books is a registered trademark, and the Circle colophon is a
trademark of Penguin Random House LLC.

Originally published in slightly different form in the United States by
Doubleday, a division of Penguin Random House LLC, New York, in 1979.
Subsequently published in paperback in the United States by Broadway
Books, an imprint of the Crown Publishing Group, a division of Penguin
Random House LLC, New York, in 2001.

Library of Congress Catalog Card Number 77-15142

ISBN 978-0-385-12838-4

Printed in the United States of America

Design by Rita Aero
Calligraphy by Shun Yu

The reproductions on pages 9, 12, 17 and 27 are from the
Avery Brundage Collection of the
Asian Art Museum of San Francisco.

40 39 38

CONTENTS

I think if we are to feel at home in the world . . . we shall have to admit Asia to equality in our thoughts, not only politically but culturally. What changes this will bring about I do not know, but I am convinced that they will be profound and of the greatest importance.

— Bertrand Russell,
History of Western Philosophy (1946)

Introduction

The book you have opened is an ancient treasure. It has been used by the Chinese to explore the meaning of human affairs for thousands of years. Translated into numerous languages, the *I Ching* continues today to be a source book of insight and wisdom for people around the world.

The *I Ching* (literally translated and used herein as *The Book of Change*) may be the oldest book on the planet. Like the Old Testament, the Pyramids, and the great Gothic cathedrals, *The Book of Change* was a co-operative effort spanning many centuries. The oldest, deepest stratum of the ideas in the book was probably handed down from the elders of the nomadic Siberian tribes, the same tribes that sired both the Oriental and American cultures. These early authors of the *I Ching* observed the stars and tides, the plants and animals, and the cycles of all natural events. At the same time, they observed the patterns of relationship in families and societies, the practice of business, the craft of government, the grim art of warfare, the eternal human dramas of love, ambition, conflict, and honor. They made no attempt to create a fixed chart of the cosmos. Instead, they organically grew a guide to the way things change: a marvelous, fluid, interconnected system of relations — the eight trigrams and the sixty-four hexagrams. It is in the simultaneous awareness of agricultural cycles and social patterns, courtly manners and battlefield strategies, cosmic events and inner development that *The Book of Change* succeeds in communicating over the millennia with such awesome accuracy.

The actual authorship of *The Book of Change* was first attributed to Fu Hsi, the legendary ruler of China during the third millennium B.C. He is said to have discovered the arrangements of the eight trigrams that form the sixty-four hexagrams on the shell of a tortoise. Early writings describe Fu Hsi's deliberations of life in the world as follows:

In the beginning there was yet no moral nor social order. Men knew their mothers only, not their fathers. When hungry, they searched for food; when satisfied, they threw away the remnants. They devoured their food, hide and hair; drank the blood; and clad themselves in skins and rushes. Then came Fu Hsi and looked upward and contemplated the images in heaven and looked downward and contemplated the occurrences on earth. He united man and wife, regulated the five stages of change, and laid down the laws of humanity. He devised the eight trigrams in order to gain mastery over the world.

Historically, *The Book of Change* was most widely used as a farming, fishing, and hunting almanac, until King Wen, founder of the Chou Dynasty (1150–249 B.C.), wrote essays on the meanings of the sixty-four hexagrams. The mythic layers of prehistoric knowledge began to blend into the long and stormy era of recorded Chinese history, as King Wen, a sophisticated, civilized, worldly figure, commented on the social and political implications of the hexagrams. He wrote his commentaries while imprisoned by the tyrannical Emperor Chou Hsin. During his confinement he saw a vision of the hexagrams on the wall of his cell, a vision so profoundly moving that he spent his sentence translating the images into words. The Judgments of King Wen were a monumental addition to the already ancient hexagrams, for the worlds of commerce, politics, and social relations were brought into relation with the elemental forces of nature.

Finally, King Wen was rescued from his incarceration when his son Wu led a rebellion to overthrow Chou Hsin. King Wen took the throne, and his son, now the Duke of Chou, completed his father's work by writing commentaries on each of the six lines within the hexagrams.

The most distinguished philosophers of Chinese thought, including Lao Tzu, Mencius, Mo Tzu, Chu Hsi, and Chuang Tzu, have been influenced by *The Book of Change* and have also influenced the book through their own works. The most important contribution among these was a series of commentaries about the hexagrams and some of the individual lines written by the revered philosopher Confucius (551–479 B.C.) and his disciples. Confucius' selection of writings about the work, known as the *Ten Wings*, is an indispensable treatise for the serious student who desires an increased insight into the *I Ching*.

Lo P'ing (1733-1799) is best known for his paintings of Buddhist and Taoist figures. He entitles this portrait of a Taoist god, "Picture of a Lofty Figure among Heavenly Clouds."

Beyond seeing *The Book of Change* as a tapestry of history, governmental policy, philosophy, morality, ethics, and an almanac of tools, farming, weather, and science, Confucius believed in using the book as a credo to determine and define his inner development. He said, "Instead of indulging in empty talk, I consider it more meaningful and enlightening to express myself in definite actions." He spent the later part of his life studying and experimenting with *The Book of Change* and is said to have worn out three times the leather thongs holding together the parchment upon which it was written. Confucius was also said to have lamented that if he had another fifty years to live, he would study the *I* (change), and in doing so, avoid great error and become without fault.

The startling accuracy of the psychological portraits presented by each of the sixty-four hexagrams was the aspect of *The Book of Change* that so excited psychologist Carl Jung, who came across Richard Wilhelm's translation in the early part of this century. Jung was so impressed and intrigued by what he saw that he convinced a wealthy patient and her husband, a scion of the Mellon family, to underwrite the publication of the American edition. Jung realized that the Chinese sages were well aware of the mythic consciousness attached to their heroes and villains, gods and kings, warriors and statesmen. He saw human nature and cosmic order united in the collective unconscious through symbols that affect people of any time and of any culture. The *I Ching* organized these vital symbols into *hexagrams;* Jung called them *archetypes.*

The Book of Change has been used throughout time to isolate the present moment and predict the future. Using *The Book of Change* for divination by dropping three coins on a flat surface six times or randomly dividing fifty small sticks of wood is a way of stopping the world, or time. Think of it as clicking the shutter of a camera in order to capture a picture of the moment and examine in detail its meaning. This ritual of stopping time (or "change," if you will) with a particular question in mind is a way of aligning your Self and your circumstances within the background of all that is unfolding in the universe. You can then use this perspective to gain an insight into your own destiny. When you use *The Book of Change* to peer into your future, when you experience the immediateness of your situation through divination, it is like unwrapping, unfolding, and discovering yourself — and, in the process, discovering this intricate and perplexing world to be something that you have intimately understood all along.

In this late Manchu illustration, the legendary Emperor Yao, active around 2357 B.C., is commissioning his scholars to organize the calendar and pay respect to the movements of the heavenly bodies.

CHAPTER I

The Book of Change Explained

11

The Tao

There is nothing constant in the universe. All ebb and flow, and every shape that's born, bears in its womb the seeds of change.

—Ovid, *Metamorphoses*

The search for a solution to the mystery underlying the constant motion and change in the universe has spawned both the science of physics and the earlier science of metaphysics. Physics attempts to express mathematically the physical laws dominating the universe. Metaphysics attempts to express mathematically the effects of these physical laws on human affairs. There are two fundamental laws underlying physical change in the universe. One is the law of *polar reversal*. In all things we see the seeds of their opposites: Just as new life carries in its genetic code the signal for its own decomposition, so too in every human affair lies the seed of a subtle but exacting change. The other law of change is *periodicity*. This law manifests in cycles and rhythms, like the changing seasons, the growth cycles in plants, and the stages in the development of the individual's life and character.

The whole of all that is changing according to these physical laws of the universe, from the life forms on earth to the stars above, is referred to herein as the cosmos. The path of life through the changing cosmos is the *tao*. The *tao* is the only reasonable and harmonious path for the individual through the cosmos, given his nature and the nature of the cosmic forces at a given moment in time. Hence, the great concern of following the *tao* in Chinese philosophical thought.

The *tao* literally means the way or gate through which all things move. To move with the *tao* is to be in a state that Christianity refers to as "grace." The Chinese philosophers were fond of comparing *taoist* behavior with that of water: It flows onward always. It penetrates the crevices, it wears down resistance, it stops to fill deep places and then flows on. Always it holds to its true nature and always it flows with the forces in the cosmos.

Although the *tao* implies the path of least resistance, it is often a very difficult path to accept and follow. In following the *tao*, the individual can find his place in the cosmos and harmonize with it. At this point he can exercise true free will as he makes *real* decisions based upon *real* possibilities. Here *The Book of Change* can illuminate the individual by revealing immediate tendencies in the cosmos. Confucius wrote in the *Ten Wings*, "Whoever knows the *tao* of the changes and transformations, knows the actions of the gods."

The contemplation of water is a common Taoist theme in Chinese painting. Here three scholars are looking at a waterfall in this striking finger-painting entitled "Three Laughing Friends," by Kao Ch'i-p'ei (1672-1734).

YIN	YANG
negative	positive
passive	active
female	male
receptive	creative
dark	light
night	day
cold	heat
soft	hard
wet	dry
winter	summer
shadow	sun

Yin and Yang

Most Westerners are familiar with the above symbol, as it appears often in both Oriental art and in modern Western illustrations. It represents the duality in the cosmos as it pulls apart into negative and positive, *yin* and *yang*. As *The Book of Change* relates it, the cosmos, desiring to manifest itself, divided its nature into two opposing forces. From the oscillating dichotomy in its nature (negative *yin* and positive *yang),* all of that which exists is being produced. The dots in the centers of the white-and-black fields represent the seeds of change as polar reversal and periodicity occur. This constant changing is the interplay in the cosmos that creates life, while life, in turn, generates the creative energy that manifests the cosmos.

Yin and *yang* represent the negative and positive dualism existing within all things, from the protons and electrons of the atoms to the conscious and subconscious of the human psyche. This duality is a profound fundamental in both ancient Chinese and modern scientific thought. In *The Book of Change,* yin and yang are represented by yielding *(yin)* and firm *(yang)* lines. They have the following attributes:

Together, *yin* and *yang* represent the dynamic interaction that creates all of reality. The ancient Chinese say about this: "From the Creative *(yang)* and the Receptive *(yin)* emerge the ten thousand things."

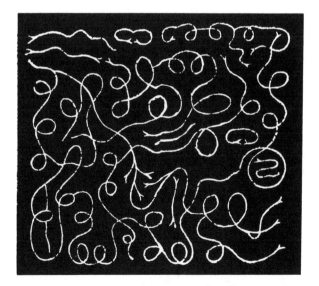

From the Northern Sung Dynasty, this illustration is referred to as the "Diagram of Change." It shows the action of the tao *and the dynamic interaction of microcosm and macrocosm.*

The Trigrams

A trigram is a structure composed of three parallel lines. The trigrams were formed to describe the evolution of things from the duality of *yin* and *yang*. They were first attributed to Fu Hsi, the legendary King of China, who lived sometime around 3000 B.C. His colorful history tells of his discovery of the trigrams on the shell of a horse dragon (tortoise) he found emerging from the Yellow River, where he had gone to meditate upon the meaning of life. He drew, from the markings on the tortoise, a document known as the Yellow River Map. From it he developed the mathematical ordering of the trigrams.

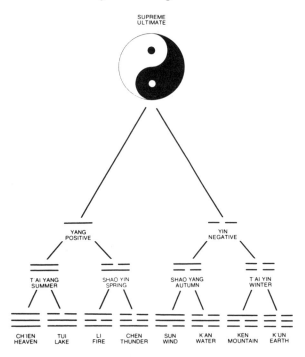

The above illustration shows the evolution of the eight trigrams emerging from the Supreme Ultimate, the absolute. The two top lines represent the duality in nature, *yin* and *yang,* or heaven and earth. The middle row shows the four ways heaven and earth come together forming the four seasons. In the bottom row, a third line was added to represent man as the synthesis of heaven and earth, thus creating the eight elemental trigrams. These trinities are meant to represent all the cosmic and physical conditions on earth. Their attributes as used in *The Book of Change* are as follows:

CH'IEN: (Heaven) firmness, creativity, strength, force, power

TUI: (Lake) joy, openness, pleasure, satisfaction, excess

LI: (Fire) Illuminating, clarity, intelligence, dependence, attachment

CHEN: (Thunder) arousing, movement, activity, shock, growth

SUN: (Wind) gentle effects, small efforts, penetrating work

K'AN: (Water) mysterious, profound, meaningful, dangerous, difficult

KEN: (Mountain) still, resting, meditating, tranquil, immobile

K'UN: (Earth) yielding, receptive, responsive, devoted, submissive

The trigrams were used in early forms of divination, before the hexagrams were created. The following illustration, found on artifacts of great antiquity throughout the Orient, was used for divination.

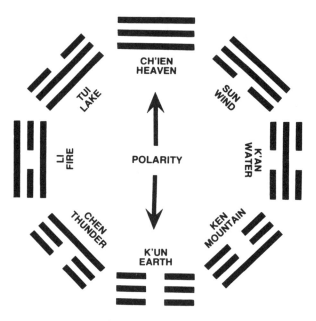

Attributed to Fu Hsi, this illustration represents the earliest arrangement of the trigrams. It depicts them in such a way that the polar opposites are across from one another. Moving clockwise from the top, heaven is across from earth, wind from thunder, water from fire, and mountain from lake. They also have the respective attributes of firm across from yielding, gentle from arousing, mysterious from illuminating, and stillness from joyfulness. A later arrangement, attributed to King Wen, shows the trigrams from the point of view of periodicity rather than polarity. You will find on page 162 a comparison of the two.

Finally, the trigrams are also seen as family members in their various archetypal roles: the strong father, the devoted mother, the arousing eldest son, the dangerous middle son, the resting youngest son, the gentle eldest daughter, the intelligent middle daughter, and the joyful youngest daughter.

Historically, the eight trigrams have been expressed in many other sets of ideas, ideas that correspond to the seasons, parts of the body, points of the compass, plants, animals, and so forth, hence creating a useful almanac and oracle for the ancient Chinese seeking to understand the tendencies of change.

Fu Hsi inventing the eight trigrams.

The Hexagrams

The eight trigrams were a manageable number of configurations that could easily be recognized and memorized. They were developed and contemplated for centuries until early Chinese scholars, desiring a more sophisticated method of investigation into the universe, combined them to expand the possible representation of cosmic and human affairs. The various pairings of the eight trigrams led to the sixty-four hexagrams: 8 × 8 = 64. The coming together of the two trigrams within the hexagrams represents the coming together of heaven (upper) and earth (lower), while their interaction and dynamism represent the cosmic forces as they affect human affairs. This coming together also represents the duality within the Self: subconscious vs. conscious or instinct vs. persona. Often the upper and lower trigrams within the hexagrams are viewed as the higher and lower minds, while in the *Workbook* they are referred to as *cosmic ideals* and *human affairs*. When contemplating the meaning of a hexagram, it should be considered in the light of the trigrams that form it and their relative positions.

The *changing lines* came about because of the recognition by the ancient Chinese that the cosmos is in a constant state of change, from night to day, summer to winter, life to death. The hexagams, therefore, flow into one another through various moving lines that occur during divination. These transformations can be expressed mathematically as: 64 × 64 = 4,096 possible permutations against a background of unlimited cosmic situations.

All movement enters the hexagram from the bottom; hence the bottom line represents the beginning of the situation. It moves upward through the

various states of conditioned change, exiting from the top, the final stage of the situation that the hexagram represents. For this reason the hexagram is always constructed from the bottom up when divining.

Each hexagram contains one and sometimes two *ruling lines*. The ruler is most commonly found in the fifth position, but its actual place, finally, depends on the suitability of the surrounding lines within the hexagram. The suitability or *correctness* of the lines is a complex subject that may take years of contemplation to fully understand. The interpretation in Book Three of *The Book of Changes*, translated by Richard Wilhelm, can be invaluable in this pursuit, as can the James Legge translation.

The overall *sequence* of the hexagrams, from one to sixty-four, can lend insight into their individual meanings. By considering the hexagrams that precede and that follow a certain hexagram, one can gain a perspective of its essence. The King Wen sequence is the order in which the hexagrams have been arranged since the twelfth century, when King Wen wrote his commentary and reorganized them. An illustration of this sequence can be found on page 163.

Duke Feng-kuo (1085-1147) passed into history as an implacable defender of Chinese territory and as one of the main proponents of Neo-Confucianism.

C H A P T E R II

Using *The Book of Change* to Forecast Events

This ancient tortoise shell was used as an augury. The shell was heated until it cracked and the cracks were then interpreted. The inscriptions refer to the inquiry and the answer. The most common questions concerned matters of sacrifice, war, hunting, trips, and weather, in that order.

How the Oracle Works

Man has used auguries throughout time to examine his reality and divine its meanings, auguries such as tea leaves, heavenly bodies, bones, tarot cards, pendulums, the palms of hands, and crystal balls. An augury is a device that yields a particular pattern at a particular moment in time and that can, in turn, be analyzed in the light of a particular concern. Imagine, for a moment, our reality to be a tube of time extending through space. We are constantly flowing through the tube along with everything we perceive. Now, if we could at a certain, perhaps perplexing moment, slice through the tube and study its fixed cross section, we would see all of the elements in nature that happen to now exist, as well as their immediate relationships to one another. By evaluating the patterns of the current relationships among things, we should then be able to divine what we might expect in our own lives from the available forces and compelling tendencies in the cosmos.

This method of investigation into things interestingly parallels the random principle used in quantum physics today. Here a random event is juxtaposed against a fixed system of physical laws in order to expand the conceptual awareness of the investigating scientist. *The Book of Change* is the oldest continuing system of investigation into the nature of the universe. Beyond its regard for human affairs, it was first used to measure time and the seasons, investigate phenomena in nature, and regulate the life forms used for food. With it, the individual investigator and his tools of divination (most often three coins) provided the random principle juxtaposed against a highly precise binary grid of the 64 hexagrams and their 4,096 mathematically exact interrelationships.

You and your sincere quest for information will become, through the random pattern of the falling coins, a microcosm juxtaposed against and created by the macrocosm of the universe. As above, so below. Just as the movements of the heavenly bodies resemble the movements within the atom, so your situation on earth resembles and is a product of the momentarily simultaneous physical forces in the universe that allow the coins to fall as they do. By building a hexagram with the six falls of the coins and referring to its text in *The Book of Change,* you are presented with a glimpse of these parallel universal patterns.

The *Workbook* you are holding will guide you through the laboratory of the universe. *You* are the investigator, and the experiments that you make and record in this book will eventually lead you to a greater understanding of the cosmos and your Self, one and the same.

At times in your life you may use *The Book of Change* quite frequently, especially in the beginning of your relationship with this highly personalized and sometimes eccentric oracle. At other times you may pick up the book only once or twice a month. For some people, years pass before they renew an animated relationship with the book. For still others, *The Book of Change* becomes a morning ritual, like coffee. "What will the day bring?" they ask. This type of relationship is an effective learning tool and can be highly entertaining as well as enlightening. An interesting and useful structure for such inquiries is presented in *The Taoist Book of Days* (Ballantine Books).

Most people, however, settle into a random pattern of inquiry. When life gets hectic and confusing the book is off the bookshelf and open for weeks on end. When everyday life assumes a predictable pattern, the book is consulted only when the user is confronted by particularly perplexing problems. When life becomes busy and exciting, the book collects dust on the shelf, forgotten and usually remembered only by the most curious of moods. And one day, perhaps, you will consult the oracle knowing that it is the last time you will wish to do so. But you will soon discover all of this for yourself.

Making An Inquiry

Wording your inquiry and writing it down is a necessary part of the process of divination. It will settle your mind into the proper frame of receptivity and, at the same time, it is an effective form of self therapy. In discovering what it is you really wish to know, you learn something of your true feelings. For instance, you may inquire into the possibility of a relationship with a particular person, but in wording the question and applying a time factor to it (for example, its significance to your past, your present, your immediate future, the rest of your life, or the whole of your life), you may discover that you do not imagine the relationship extending endlessly into your future, but see it more as a thing of the present, or vice versa.

As you learn to better focus your questions, the answers you receive will become more to the point. As a rule, be as specific as possible about the time, the tense, the people involved, the place, and the scope of what you wish revealed (for example, the effect of a particular action, the best attitude to maintain in order to achieve a particular aim, what to expect from a particular situation, the current meaning of a particular situation, or the true motives in yourself or others). Especially avoid yes/no or either/or kinds of questions. "To be or not to be" is not really a question. It's indecision.

An equivocal or vague question such as "Should I move to another city?" will yield a vague response. If a more pointed response is desired, word the question, "What will be the effect of moving to Portland?" Or even better, "How will a move to Portland affect my career?" Or "What effect will a move to Portland in August have upon my life?" Here the question is developed into a state of mind.

To approach *The Book of Change* as though it were an intelligent, sensitive, living mind is not at all a mistake. John Blofeld, in his translation of the *I Ching,* (E.P. Dutton & Company), describes his first divination:

> The very first time I did this, I was overawed to a degree that amounted to fright, so strong was the impression of having received an answer to my question from a living, breathing person. I have scarcely used it since without recovering something of that awe, although it soon came to be characterized by a pleasurable excitement rather than fear. Of course I do not mean to assert that the white pages covered with black printer's ink do in fact house a lively spiritual being. I have dwelt at some length on the astounding effect they produce chiefly as a means of emphasizing how extraordinarily accurate and, so to speak, personal, are its answers in most cases. Yet, if I were asked to assert that the printed pages do not form the dwelling of a spiritual being or at least bring us into contact with one by some mysterious process, I think I should be about as hesitant as I am to assert the contrary.

Questions dealing with health, relationships, business, politics, travel, social events, and inner development have been asked of *The Book of Change* for thousands of years. Consequently, the various commentaries throughout history, from which this version was synthesized, touch upon all of these human affairs. Other more profound and rare questions, questions that are usually asked only once, questions of one's personal fate, deeply significant life decisions, or inquiries of fixed relativity between one's Self and an external are also within the scope of what *The Book of Change* will address. Such inquiries should wait until one has a careful understanding of the ideas behind the text, and has delved more deeply into the philosophical and scientific works on the *I Ching.* Additionally, it is a good idea to keep in mind that, just as the great secret of wisdom is knowing when *not* to act, there are times when one should *not* consult this oracle; there are questions that do *not* need to be asked.

Once you've formulated your question, turn to the Hexagram Journal in the back of this book, write it down, and date it. It should be short and concise. As you record it, try to get an image of your question in your mind, a face or mannerism, a room or city, an object or action, or whatever. Hold the image in your mind, have the book in front of you or on your lap, and begin forming the hexagram that represents your reality at this particular moment in time.

If you need a more structured ritual to put your mind into a properly receptive state, then use whatever kind of ceremony that works for you. For a detailed description of ritualized divination, see *The I Ching and You* by Diana ffarington Hook (E.P. Dutton & Company). However, if your attention span is under control yet flexible, in keeping with the spirit of the *tao,* you should be able to consult *The Book of Change* freely, under any circumstance.

Generally, the occult is taken for granted in the East. All events can be seen as auguries, and true wisdom lies in divining their meaning. The Eastern mind perceives the individual as a part of the continuous whole of reality. Just as a stone falling to the earth may change the molecules in the sun, so too an overt action by an individual yields a corresponding reaction somewhere down the line.

Throwing the Coins

There are many methods of divination that are used to construct a hexagram. The oldest of these is an involved system of counting fifty yarrow stalks from the plant *Achillea millefolium*. This method takes about thirty minutes and is favored by many translators of *The Book of Change*. A detailed description of the yarrow stalk method can be found in the *I Ching*, by John Blofeld (E. P. Dutton & Company).

Still other methods involve six wands, colored beads, preprogrammed calculators and computers, along with the multifarious fauna and flora of the occult world. You will eventually find your own favorite method of generating randomness, if you do not already have one. For those who are just beginning, one of the older and more popular methods here and in China is the coin method, for it is the most accessible and certainly the simplest to grasp.

To use the coin method, you will need three coins of the same size. Pennies will do very well. Have ready your pencil and paper, your question, and your powers of concentration. Cup the pennies in your hands, shake them, and drop them on a flat surface. The first fall of the three coins represents the bottom line of the hexagram. Read the coins as follows:*

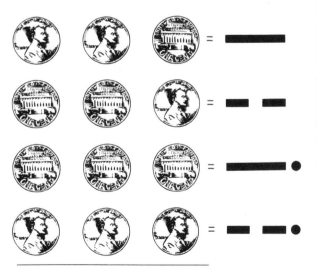

---

* The different sides of the coins are used to generate a binary code. Should the reader wish to reverse the values shown here, that is his decision.

Draw the corresponding line and repeat five more times until you have built, **from the bottom up,** a complete hexagram.

If the hexagram that you have received does not have a changing line or lines (a yielding or firm line followed by a dot), then it is a static hexagram, implies a fixed situation, and only one hexagram is read. Especially refer to the last paragraph of the text of the hexagram, since this describes its static state.

If one or more of the lines are changing, two hexagrams will result. For example, a changing firm line (——•) is read as a firm line in the first hexagram and then reversed to a yielding line (— —) in the resulting second hexagram. All other unchanging lines remain the same in the second hexagram. The illustration below will serve as an example:

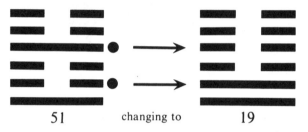

51   changing to   19

Imagine you received hexagram No. 51 as illustrated here. Counting from the bottom up, the second and fourth lines are changing lines. These two lines are therefore reversed as you draw next to No. 51 the resulting hexagram, No. 19.

When reading the text, first read hexagram No. 51. This describes the basic situation or attitude pertaining to your inquiry. It usually refers to the very recent past* or present time. Next read the text for the two changing lines, the second and the fourth. They are read and generally occur in the order in which they are received. These lines may describe the reasons for the coming change, they may present advice for the attainment of your goals, or they may be warnings of coming difficulties or auguries of good fortune. Finally, read the resulting hexagram, No. 19. This hexagram will

---

* In describing the moment in time to which a divined hexagram refers, Richard Wilhelm writes in the Introduction to his translation of *The Book of Changes:*

> . . . every event in the visible world is the effect of an 'image,' that is, of an idea in the unseen world. Accordingly, everything that happens on earth is only a reproduction, as it were, of an event in a world beyond our sense perception; as regards its occurrence in time, it is later than the suprasensible event.

describe the coming tendencies in your current or proposed path. **Do not read any changing lines in the second hexagram.**

To determine the number of the hexagrams you receive, consult the chart below. Since the hexagram is read from the bottom line up, the lower three lines make up the lower trigram, and the top three, the upper. For example, you can find hexagram No. 14 ⚍ by dividing it into (lower) and (upper).

Look down the left-hand column and locate the lower trigram, *CH'IEN,* and move across the column until you are under the upper trigram, *LI.* Here you will find No. 14. Another copy of this chart is printed on the last page of this book for easy access.

UPPER TRIGRAM ▷ / LOWER TRIGRAM ▽	CH'IEN	CHEN	K'AN	KEN	K'UN	SUN	LI	TUI
CH'IEN	1	34	5	26	11	9	14	43
CHEN	25	51	3	27	24	42	21	17
K'AN	6	40	29	4	7	59	64	47
KEN	33	62	39	52	15	53	56	31
K'UN	12	16	8	23	2	20	35	45
SUN	44	32	48	18	46	57	50	28
LI	13	55	63	22	36	37	30	49
TUI	10	54	60	41	19	61	38	58

Interpreting the Answer

In the East, scholars and novice practitioners of *The Book of Change* are required to memorize the whole of the text and the meaning of its sequence long before divination is ever attempted. To pore over the book and study the different hexagrams, both at random and in sequence, would certainly further one's ability to interpret. This is particularly true if you decide to use the Wilhelm, Blofeld, Legge, or Z. D. Sung editions, which are more or less direct translations. The *Workbook*, however, is a synthesis of these translations and many other interpretations, written with an eye to the relevant semantics of modern Western languages. Much of the work of making the universal images of the hexagrams apparent and distinct is done for you. The spirit of the *Workbook* is one of learning by doing; therefore, you should be able to readily find your way into the midst of this vast subject. After you have developed a rapport with *The Book of Change*, which is the goal in presenting this format, you are encouraged to approach the aforementioned books in order to expand your understanding of the symbology, mythic experiences, and collective awareness common to all of mankind.

The Book of Change is an eccentric oracle. Anyone who has used it for any length of time will discover that it has a distinct personality. It could be that it takes on the personality of the user, although it frequently assumes a startling and unpredictable posture. Sometimes it likes to carry on a witty and multifaceted conversation; and at other times it petulantly dwells upon a particular issue or problem. If you ask the same question over and over again, it often gives you the same advice couched in various nuances. At other times it may become irritable and insulting when you importune. As a rule, the answer you receive will be as clear and comprehensive as your question and frame of mind. It is a good practice to briefly note the answer in a few words under your question. Then, when you next return to the book, after the situation has resolved itself, you can re-evaluate the true meaning of your hexagram. In this way, you will enhance your understanding of the personalized language you are developing with *The Book of Change*.

Keep in mind, too, that *The Book of Change* may not directly answer your question but may, instead, address itself to your motives or subconscious urges in asking. Or, sensing a coming crisis or significant change, the oracle may take the opportunity of the conversation you've initiated to alert you. You may find it a willful book — neither to be put off nor to be used aimlessly. As your relationship with *The Book of Change* becomes more sophisticated, it may embarrass you, startle you, tease you, frighten you, and occasionally share a good laugh with you.

Your rapport with *The Book of Change* is primarily based upon your ability to understand its language and "converse" with it. For example, K was intrigued by a new friend who had left on a trip shortly after they met. She inquired of *The Book of Change,* "What can I accomplish in a relationship with T?" She received hexagram No. 1, CREATIVE POWER, changing to No. 44, TEMPTATION. The first line of CREATIVE POWER was changing, suggesting that the time was not at all right for action, and that there were conflicting motives involved in the as yet undeveloped relationship. K then changed her tack and asked, "What is it you are trying to tell me?" She received hexagram No. 32, CONTINUING, changing to No. 50, COSMIC ORDER. Here *The Book of Change* suggested that she adhere to traditional values (CONTINUING). It further advised that she not wear herself out with restless anxieties (top changing line of CONTINUING), and promised eventual peace of mind if she aligned herself realistically with the flow of the times and behaved in a consonant manner with the situation at hand (COSMIC ORDER). Weeks later, when the interrupted relationship resumed, it ran into complex difficulties based upon unfortunate timing in both of their lives. In a matter of days, they again found themselves in different cities. CREATIVE POWER here, clearly showed the enthusiasm of the beginning, but the unfortunate changing line, in the bottom position of the very beginning of things, changed the whole situation to one of inappropriate TEMPTATION. Yet, the advice on her second inquiry, CONTINUING changing to COSMIC ORDER, was a truly sympathetic response.

The question of whether the augury comes from the subconscious of K, from an actual entity in the book, or from a curious, coincidental device seems unimportant in the light of its actual usefulness and often startling accuracy. Richard Wilhelm, in the Introduction to his translation of *The Book of Changes*, attempts to explain this startling phenomenon using the metaphor of electricity:

> The way in which *The Book of Changes* works can best be compared to an electrical circuit reaching into all situations. The circuit only affords the potentiality of lighting; it

does not give light. But when contact with a definite situation is established through the questioner, the 'current' is activated, and the given situation is illuminated.

Possibly you may find an answer you receive to be too complex and seemingly contradictory. This may happen because the extenuating circumstances surrounding your affairs are more intricately conditioned than you might realize. If you receive an answer that you cannot penetrate, try dividing your question into two or more parts. For instance, the question "What can I expect if I go to Los Angeles to work with M on my project?" yielded hexagram No. 23, DETERIORATION, changing to No. 14, SOVEREIGNTY. How could this be? Does the DETERIORATION come in the process of traveling to Los Angeles, or is it connected to the project and M's help? And what is implied by the very good omen of SOVEREIGNTY? To help clarify the interpretation, the question was divided into two parts: "What will be the effect of working with M on my project?" and "What can be expected in traveling to Los Angeles in August?" The coins were thrown and the final answers indicated that it would be a very good thing, indeed, to work with M on the project (Hexagram No. 11, PROSPERING), but that traveling to Los Angeles would create difficulties that were undesirable considering what needed to be accomplished (hexagram No. 64, BEFORE THE END, changing to No. 21, REFORM). The point at where the advice is actually applied, of course, is where *The Book of Change* ends and your work begins.

In interpreting your answers, wishful thinking may become a major stumbling block. It is amazing what the mind can read into an omen. Wishful thinking is not a habit you can suddenly decide to eradicate from your repertoire of response, but, by remaining mindful of its presence, you can learn to become more objective and intuitive in interpreting your answers. In developing your powers of intuition, you begin to evolve your subconscious into a more sophisticated instrument of perception, able to penetrate the true forces at work in your life.

Because of the personal nature of your perceptions, you should refrain from asking questions for others. It is somewhat unfeasible to tap *your* subconscious to give meaning and illumination to another's life. Mediumship is a delicate art not given to everyone to develop, and, in any event, one begins in one's Self in matters of enlightenment.

You can, however, use the book for penetrating social, political, personal, or natural events. These events have been the major focus of *The Book of Change* throughout history, and most commentaries specifically address such issues. Carl Jung, in his works on synchronicity and the collective unconsciousness, carefully outlined the mutual participation that all of mankind has in cosmic events. Therefore, whether your inquiry is about a political election, a drought, a financial strategy, or a coming social event, *The Book of Change* has used the principles of synchronicity and the collective mind to address itself to such issues for thousands of years.

The hexagrams themselves can be analyzed by regarding the relationships of their *component* and *nuclear* trigrams. This method is the oldest and considered the most sound in penetrating the true cosmic events implied in any hexagram. The *component* trigrams point to the most dynamic external aspects at work in a given hexagram. There are two component trigrams in a hexagram, made up of lines 1, 2, and 3 and lines 4, 5, and 6 (counting from the bottom up).

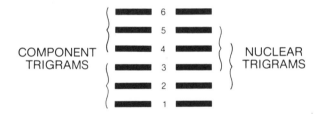

For example, in hexagram No. 43, RESOLUTION, the lower component trigram is *CH'IEN*, heaven, and the upper is *TUI*, lake.

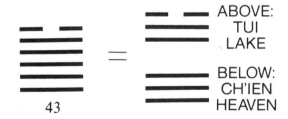

From the chart on the next page, you can see that *CH'IEN* has the attributes of strength and firmness, and *TUI*, of openness. Additionally, *CH'IEN* means head or mind, and *TUI*, mouth or words. Therefore the component trigrams point to the idea of an open, verbal, firm RESOLUTION, which is the advice given in the text.

Furthermore, by examining the two *nuclear* trigrams, lines 2, 3, and 4 and lines 3, 4, and 5 (again, counting from the bottom up), you will see a picture of the internal workings of the hexagrams. In RESOLUTION, the lower nuclear trigrams is again *CH'IEN*, heaven, as is the upper.

HEXAGRAM 43 = UPPER: CH'IEN HEAVEN / LOWER: CH'IEN HEAVEN = NUCLEAR HEXAGRAM 1

These nuclear trigrams further imply the idea of firmness, strength, high ideals, paternal moods, and untiring disciplines. By then combining them, they form hexagram No. 1, CREATIVE POWER, indicating a need for and evolution toward internal creative strength, strength of character.

The more advanced student of *The Book of Change* can develop a facile understanding of any hexagram by examining this internal hexagram resulting from the combination of the two *nuclear* trigrams. This, understandably, will come much later for the beginner. Nevertheless, both the component and the nuclear trigrams are illustrated next to the text, for easy reference.

The changing lines will describe the various aspects of the change from the first hexagram to the second. When several changing lines are received that appear to contradict one another, they should be read as sequential events in the change from one situation to the next. They may also be regarded as various points of view you may develop while in transition. A line that seems to contradict the hexagram of which it is a part should take precedence over the advice given in that hexagram. Ruling lines are marked with a ▶ next to the commentary. They tend to be more pivotal and dynamic and sometimes more auspicious than the other lines. When you receive a ruling line along with other lines, it is a good idea to place greater emphasis upon it in your mind.

TRIGRAM ATTRIBUTES

CH'IEN	HEAVEN SKY DAY	CREATIVE ENERGY STRONG LIGHT	EARLY WINTER COLD ICE	FATHER	ONENESS FIRMNESS	HEAD MIND
K'UN	EARTH NIGHT	WEAK YIELDING DARK NOURISHING	EARLY AUTUMN WARM	MOTHER	ADAPTIVE	BELLY WOMB
CHEN	THUNDER	AROUSING ACTIVE EXCITING	SPRING EARTHQUAKE	ELDEST SON	EXPANSIVE	FOOT
K'AN	WATER MOON	DANGEROUS DIFFICULT ABYSSMAL	MID WINTER CLOUDY	MIDDLE SON	ANXIOUS MELANCHOLY	EAR
KEN	MOUNTAIN	KEEPING STILL IMMOVABLE PERVERSE	LATE WINTER STILLNESS	YOUNGEST SON	CALM STUBBORN	HAND
SUN	WIND WOOD	GENTLE PENETRATING GRADUAL	EARLY SUMMER MILD MOVEMENT	ELDEST DAUGHTER	GENTLE	THIGH
LI	FIRE SUN	CONSCIOUS DEPENDING	MID SUMMER LIGHTNING	MIDDLE DAUGHTER	INTELLIGENT DEPENDENT	EYE
TUI	LAKE	JOYFUL SATISFIED FULNESS PLEASURE	LATE AUTUMN RAIN	YOUNGEST DAUGHTER	OPENNESS EXCESS	MOUTH

			ASPECT	NATURALLY CORRECT LINE POSITION
COSMIC IDEALS	6 TOP LINE	HEAVEN	WISDOM	
	5 FIFTH LINE	HEAVEN	AUTHORITY	
	4 FOURTH LINE	MAN	SOCIAL CONSCIOUSNESS	
HUMAN AFFAIRS	3 THIRD LINE	MAN	INDIVIDUAL ENDEAVORS	
	2 SECOND LINE	EARTH	SELF INTEREST	
	1 BOTTOM LINE	EARTH	INSTINCTS	

When analyzing and intuiting the meanings of the individual lines, a familiarity with the line positions and their attributes, as illustrated in the chart **above**, may be helpful in resolving more intricate divinations.

In examining the chart from left to right, you can see that lines 1, 2, and 3 are in the lower trigram of human affairs, and that lines 4, 5, and 6 are in the upper trigram of cosmic ideals. Their meanings generally correspond to these interests. The bottom two lines are often concerned with very basic matters, the middle two with social or human affairs, and the top two with higher pursuits. Each line has a specific aspect, from the bottom position of instinct to the top line of wisdom. Finally, the correct and natural position for the type of line (firm or yielding) is shown. If a line is naturally correct in the correct position, it is usually favorable, although this is somewhat modified by adjacent lines, corresponding lines (lines 1 and 4, 2 and 5, or 3 and 6), and ruling lines.

As a rule, the bottom and top lines are outside of the situation; the bottom at the very beginning, or cause, and the top at the very end, or effect. Their meanings, therefore, are often distant from the center of change. This occurs because they are each only part of one trigram. The second and fifth lines are part of two trigrams each, one component and one nuclear. Their meanings are often auspicious because they are well balanced. The two inner lines, the third and fourth, are part of three trigrams each, one component and both nuclear. Their meanings are more conditioned and involved because they are in the very center of change and dependent upon the other lines.

Keep in mind that these are only general principles and that everything depends upon the structure of the hexagram as a whole. The intricate relationships among the six lines in a given hexagram will become clear only after much contemplation. You will find, in the column next to the text of the hexagrams, useful illustrations and comments about the relationships of the lines.

When many lines are changing in the hexagram you receive, it may imply a volatile or more active and intricate change. When no lines are changing, you are in a static situation. This may refer to a fixed attitude you may have about the object of your inquiry. A static hexagram may also indicate that the circumstances surrounding your inquiry are rigid and can be overcome only through extraordinary means, or that the answer is definitive and unequivocal. The final paragraph of the text of the hexagrams deals with such "static" situations, although the entire text should be read and considered as well.

You will discover, too that your own notations in the *Workbook,* next to the individual lines, will give you increasing insight into their meanings and the meanings of the hexagrams as a whole.

The lotus is much esteemed by the Taoists and is held to be a symbol of mathematical perfection or openheartedness. This delicate silk painting is one of a set of album leaves by Yun Ping (1670-1710).

C H A P T E R III

How to Use
The I Ching Workbook

The Meeting of East and West

The German novelist, poet, and philosopher Goethe once remarked, "*Orient und Occident sind nicht mehr zu trennen.*" (East and West can no longer be kept apart.) How true this is, even in small matters! Westerners eagerly examine and experience oriental art, food, sports, music, dress, and literature. They are fascinated by the subtle variations of texture, mood and tone that make everyday life so different from their own. And yet, this unfamiliar, intriguing Eastern culture comprises a vast proportion of the population of this planet. As the earth's consciousness continues to regroup and coalesce, the peoples of the West and the East each share a growing desire to indulge in the stimulating ideas of the other.

The occult, for instance, while becoming increasingly important in serious Western philosophy, is dominated by Eastern ideas. At this time in the development of Western civilization, we feel an inner-famine, a need for greater meaning in our lives and a desire for expanded potentials in consciousness. Paradoxically, the peoples of the East desire the advanced technology that we have developed through attention to our external reality. They seek to control, as well as contemplate, the forces of nature in order to improve their physical lives.

The differences between the Eastern mind and the Western mind are profound and fascinating. These differences might be portrayed as opposites in philosophical thought. The oriental mind has been characterized by its synthetic thinking and symbolic imagination. This can readily be seen in the written languages, where the word characters symbolically depict the idea they represent.

While analytical thinking and logical reasoning have been the Western standard of thought, the people of the East have preferred to develop their powers of intuitive reasoning. An example of intuitive reasoning in a Western laboratory might be to program into the computer a bit of seemingly unrelated datum — a random pattern, so to speak, like the current phase of the moon, or the time of day when a certain decision is being made, or perhaps the biorhythms of the inquirer. To the Eastern mind, even irrelevant details are assumed to be part of the whole picture and are not necessarily isolated and investigated for their own sake. Therefore, by introducing a random element into the experiment, the Eastern experimenter would feel certain that the farthest-reaching factors of universal truth would be taken into account.

This type of reasoning is perplexing to the Western mind and sometimes threatening or repellent because it seems shrouded in mystery and thoroughly nonscientific. At the same time, Westerners are attracted to these abstract notions that sometimes startlingly reveal formerly unperceived possibilities. This provocative relationship of cultural opposites in thought may promise a proliferation of new ideas for the future.

The I Ching Workbook was developed to facilitate a Western approach to *The Book of Change* without misrepresenting the original Chinese concepts and at the same time preserving our own heritage and the tools of thought it affords us. This idea was aptly expressed by renowned psychologist, Carl Jung in the Appendix to Richard Wilhelm's translation of *The Secret of the Golden Flower* (Harcourt, Brace & World, Inc.):

We need to have a correctly three-dimensional life if we wish to experience Chinese wisdom as a living thing. Therefore we first have need of European truths about ourselves. Our way begins in European reality and not in yoga practices, which would

EARLY *DRAGON*   MODERN *DRAGON*   EARLY *FISH*   MODERN *FISH*

Modern Chinese writing finds its roots in picture or symbol writing. Here the early ideograms, known as bone writing, are shown next to their modern counterparts.

only lead us astray to our own reality. We must continue Wilhelm's work of translation in a wider sense if we wish to show ourselves worthy pupils of the master. Just as he translated the spiritual treasure of the East into European meaning, we should translate this meaning into life.

The I Ching Workbook was designed and written to encourage the Western seeker to penetrate this great work and experience it in a more familiar format. The text of the sixty-four hexagrams in the *Workbook* is not a direct translation of the original Chinese. In an attempt to bring the essence and idea of the ancient text into the light of contemporary Western understanding, the *Workbook* contains modern terminology in place of the original word symbols, the meanings of which are lost on those unfamiliar with the significance of the wild goose, the flying dragon, the withered poplar, and so forth. While some persons are gifted with mythic understanding and are quite able to comprehend fully the beautifully imagistic translations, for most the everyday catch phrases of a cultural work nearly five thousand years old are obscure. Nevertheless, the trigrams that form the hexagrams, the elements of nature they represent, and the dynamism of their juxtapositions from hexagram to hexagram are of great universal significance and are illustrated next to the text. The contemplation of these building blocks of the hexagrams, as suggested by masters of *The Book of Change*, will ultimately lead to a profound understanding of the ways in which the laws of nature affect human affairs.

In using the *Workbook* and recording within it the results of your inquiries, you will gain a personal understanding of the sixty-four human situations. As you continue to make notations of your inquiries into the future, you will create a diary and map of your path through the cosmos, the *tao*. Patterns in your life will emerge and you will notice a certain predictability in the way intricate matters resolve themselves. You will develop an acceptance of that which is fated, perceive the limits of your power to affect certain situations, and, above all, cultivate that greatest of gifts, intuition.

In order to accurately interpret *The Book of Change,* you must develop your own individual approach through the active use of intuition. In the *Workbook* you will be writing your own book, basing it upon the structure of an ancient binary system. You will be determining its meaning through the notation of actual personal experience.

Experience will be your teacher, and the *Workbook* will be the computer storing your data. With this type of learning tool, memory and recall are at hand. Your powers of observation and your awareness of tendencies will be enhanced. You will begin to note the way things usually happen to *you.* You can learn to avoid danger, to jump at opportunities, or to recognize the time for retreat. You will become more sensitive to the inner workings of your psychological makeup, and you will be presented with the opportunity to make real changes in your life or reaffirm the direction of your current path.

Glossary

These words are used frequently in the text of the hexagrams and throughout the *Workbook.* Their intended meanings are as follows:

AUTHORITY: This term and the terms *leader* and *superiors* refer to a situation or person whose decisions affect your life at a given moment in time. Also, anyone who has influence over others.

CHAOS: This term and the term *confusion* refer to a state of disorder or unconnectedness with the *tao.* In states of *chaos,* one is in danger of both spoiling the future by inappropriate action and undermining the good works of the past.

CORRECT: This term and the terms *right* and *righteous* refer to actions and attitudes that are in harmony with the environment and one's own nature: the *tao.* In doing what is *correct,* conflict is avoided. Also, this term refers to a line in an appropriate position with the hexagram.

CORRESPONDING LINES: This term refers to lines which are in identical positions in both of the component trigrams within a hexagram. *Corresponding lines* are lines 1 and 4, lines 2 and 5, and lines 3 and 6.

EVIL: This term and the terms *decadence* and *decay* refer to a compromise of principle and a moral corruption that will cause pain and confusion to everyone concerned.

FIRM: A line in the hexagram that is unbroken (——) and thus strong and determined. Also, a strong and determined attitude.

GOOD: This term and the term *good fortune* refer to a state where deeds of merit can be accomplished. This can be a situation that will have a beneficial effect for all concerned, or a person who is growing in a state of mutual benefit with his environment.

MAN: This term and the terms *he* and *his* refer to human beings of either sex.

MISFORTUNE: This term and the terms *blame* and *error* refer to circumstances that yield adverse results, often causing one humiliation or shame, which spoil the inner effects of good works.

PERSONAL DEVELOPMENT: This phrase and the phrases *inner development* and *character development* refer to the shaping and refining of an individual's virtues; the ultimate result is a superior man who can accomplish, with ease and without evil, his aims.

PRINCIPLES: See *virtue.*

SACRIFICE: Sacrifice is the surrender of something for the sake of something else. It is not necessarily a direct exchange and, therefore, requires a certain amount of faith. Most specifically, it refers to self-discipline.

STATIC: Static refers to an unchanging, fixed hexagram or situation.

SUPERIOR MAN: The term *superior man* is used in the original Chinese text of *The Book of Change* to indicate a person striving to live his life in the best possible way. Lao Tzu, philosopher of the sixth century B.C., describes this man as follows:

> The best man is like water.
> Water is good; it benefits all things and
>   does not compete with them.
> It dwells in lowly places that all disdain.
> This is why it is so near to *tao.*
> The best man in his dwelling loves the earth.
> In his heart, he loves what is profound.
> In his associations, he loves humanity.
> In his words, he loves faithfulness.
> In government, he loves order.
> In handling of affairs, he loves competence.
> In his activities, he loves timeliness.
> It is because he does not compete that he is
>   above reproach.

The term *superior man* is replaced often by the term *you,* since it is assumed that the user of the *Workbook* has this ideal in mind.

TAO: The *tao* refers to one's personal path through the cosmos. Also, see page 12.

VIRTUE: The terms *virtue* and *principles* refer to a sincere commitment to one's standards and ethics. The man of *virtue* will remain steadfast in his principles and integrity. This is felt to be of vast importance in *The Book of Change.*

YIELDING: The term *yielding* refers to a line in the hexagram that is broken (— —), thus responsive and receptive. Also, a receptive attitude.

Making Notations in the *Workbook*

The *Workbook* is designed in such a way that after a certain amount of use, patterns in your life will begin to reveal themselves. For this reason, only you should make notations in your book. Furthermore, by making the various notations outlined below, you can gain a quick and highly personalized understanding of what certain hexagrams and lines mean in your life.

Two pages are devoted to each hexagram. On the *left-hand page* is the text of the hexagram. The names of the hexagrams are not necessarily direct translations, but instead, modern interpretations of the original concept. When these differ greatly, the most common translation can be found, in italics, under the hexagram name. For instance, hexagram No. 21, illustrated on the next page, has the title REFORM. Under the title, in parentheses, you will find its most commonly accepted direct translation, *Biting Through.*

The text of the hexagram explains how that particular hexagram affects human affairs, while the last paragraph of the text discusses its meaning when it is received in a static form (without changing lines). The trigrams that form the hexagram, and their effect upon each other, are also referred to here.

The column running down the left side of the page, next to the text, has been designed to aid those who desire to further their understanding of *The Book of Change.* At the top of the column is the hexagram number, followed by the hexagram itself. Under that is its Chinese name. The two component trigrams and the two nuclear trigrams, along with their names and meanings, come next. For a more detailed description of the aspects of the trigrams, see the chart on page 24. For thousands of years, scholars have studied the hexagrams by analyzing the relationships between the trigrams that form them.

Finally, at the bottom of the page is the hexagram again, this time with the ruling line or lines indicated. Under this is a short explanation of the structure of the hexagram.

On the *right-hand page,* below, are the changing lines and the columns in which you make your notations. The changing lines are ordered so that the bottom line appears on the bottom of the page. When you receive two or more lines, you should begin at the lowest line and read upward.

In the first column, Column A, you make a

notation each time you receive that particular hexagram in its static form. By putting a zero in the column, you can see at a glance how often you receive this hexagram, as compared to the others, in an unchanging form. The frequent occurrence of a particular static hexagram can tell you about your attitude or tendency in regard to the human situation it represents. In the case of REFORM, for example, it would suggest that there are specific tensions in your life that have not been removed or reformed.

In Column B you record the hexagrams to which that particular hexagram changes. In the example, for instance, you can see that REFORM seems to change quite often to hexagram No. 27, NOUR-ISHING. This would suggest that this person finds his way out of a blocked situation by altering his input habits or by supporting and NOURISHING others who can help him.

In Column C you make notations of changing lines received concerning often asked or significant questions. You do not use this column for all in-quiries, only those that have special meaning for you. These notations should be brief, just a word

or two, and preceded by the date (month and year). In this way you can refer to the actual question in the "Hexagram Journal" at the end of the book and study it at a later time to see how it ultimately resolved itself. This should give you a clearer un-derstanding of any particular line. You might, at this point, wish to make your own notations near the text of the lines, in order to alter the commen-tary presented in the *Workbook*. In the example, for instance, the user has several entries in Column C, next to the fifth changing line, concerning a relationship with S.M. Although it may seem un-usual, any long-term user of *The Book of Change* has experienced such striking repetitions. The meaning of the line, in this instance, is that the relationship with S.M. is continually an obstacle for the user. He has difficulty making a decision to REFORM the relationship, even though it is absolutely necessary according to the text of the hexagram. His own note in the margin, "Reform is vital!," indicates his true relationship to the line, for future reference. Much later in time, you will notice, he received both this line and the bottom line concerning a traffic violation. There was little

21

SHIH HO

**ABOVE: LI
FIRE**

**BELOW: CHEN
THUNDER**

**UPPER: K'AN
WATER**

**LOWER: KEN
MOUNTAIN**

RULING LINES

Seen similarly to hexagram No. 27, as an open mouth, the fourth line is a blockage that must be removed. Also, it prevents the two nuclear trigrams from being recep-tive. The yielding ruler must be prodded into reforming the situation.

REFORM
(BITING THROUGH)

The time calls for energetic *REFORM*. Either an inferior person who is working against you or a situation that has developed at cross purposes to your life is inter-fering with the attainment of your aims. These obstacles must be sought out, re-formed, and thereby eliminated. Success will come through the enforcement of laws and the administering of justice. There is neither possibility of compromise nor hope that the problem will miraculously vanish. It cannot be rationalized or ignored, and you cannot maneuver around it. It is a tangible, real, and self-generating interference in your life, and must be severely reformed before it causes any permanent damage to you.

In dealing with social and political affairs, a strict adherence to established justice is necessary. A society without principles or clarity about its laws is a group of people who are going nowhere. If you are a leader, then take the initiative to administer just, reasonable, and swift penalties to restore order; if you are a member, now is the time to support superior persons who can bring about social *REFORM*.

Personal relationships without defined guidelines, reasonable expectations, re-ciprocal considerations, and clear plans for the future are now in danger of dissolv-ing in the chaos being generated by the current situation. Misunderstandings and confusions will become more common unless firm, clear headed action is taken to dispense with whatever you perceive to be an obstacle to union. There are times to avoid confrontations, to sublimate deep feelings, or to retreat and await a more opportune moment for action. This is not one of those times. Energetic *REFORM* will bring favorable results.

There could not be a more appropriate time to examine your character and determine the extent to which any delusions, rationalizations, or habits have usurped control of your judgment. Equivocal or vague principles, as a rule, will make of your life an undirected, uninspired, meaningless act. Know what you want, know what makes you feel good about your Self, know what brings you into harmony with others. These are your guidelines and principles. Other factors that assume control of your behavior or your health or that create inner discord are the obstacles that must be overcome. Be firm, unemotional, gentle, and clear in annihilating them and there-by *re-forming* your Self and your environment.

There is an inner storm that has been raging for some time around the object of your inquiry. *The lower trigram, CHEN, movement, is struggling upward, sparking brilliance in the upper trigram, LI. This dramatic coming together of the two strong elemental forces creates a tremendous cacophony and, eventually, release, just as thunder and lightning bring the release of static tensions before a storm. Without changing lines, a radical REFORM is necessary in your life. It will cause spectacular reaction but will release the tensions that hold you back from your aims.*

A	B	C	D	
0	56		✓	**TOP LINE** A person who cannot recognize his own wrongdoings will drift farther and farther from the path. A person who is no longer on the path cannot understand the warnings of others. The original text states: "There will be evil."
0	14			
0	27			
0	10			
0	35			
0	27			
	20			
	12	9-76 *S. M.*	✓✓	▶**FIFTH LINE** Even though there are few alternatives, a decision is difficult to make. Once you choose the course you will take, do not waver from your decision. Remain aware of the dangers and in this way you will surmount them. *Reform is vital!*
	27	11-76 *stocks*	✓✓	
	16	2-77 *S. M.*		
	27	5-77 *S. M.*		
	35	12-77 *traffic ticket*		
	64			
	6			
	33	6-77 *quit job*	✓✓	**FOURTH LINE** The task facing you is indeed difficult. That which you must overcome is in a powerful position. Be firm and persevering once you begin. Good results come only by being alert and exercising continuous effort.
	23	2-78 *return heirloom*	✓	
	25			
		5-78 *Move to Wash.*	✓ ✓	**THIRD LINE** You lack sufficient power and authority to bring about *REFORM*. Your attempts meet with indiffer-ence, and you may feel humiliated at your ineffective actions. Yet *REFORM* is necessary, and therefore your endeavors are justified.
		11-76 *Lost papers* 1-77 *illness*	✓✓	**SECOND LINE** Punishment and retribution come swiftly and thor-oughly to the person who continues in wrong behav-ior. Even though it may seem overly severe, it will effectively bring about *REFORM*. Finally, there is no mistake in this.
		4-77 *career change* 8-77 *S. M.* 12-77 *traffic ticket* 5-78 *Move to Wash.*	✓✓ ✓✓ ✓ ✓	**BOTTOM LINE** Since this is only your first departure from the right path, only a mild punishment is forthcoming. This should serve the purpose of early *REFORM*.

question in his mind that it would be necessary to change his driving habits (Reform is vital!), but he was assured that his penalty would be just and mild (bottom line).

Finally, in Column D, you make a mark each time you receive any particular changing line. Many users of *The Book of Change* do this as a matter of course. One of the unusual aspects in divination is that, although one would assume that the lines would be evenly distributed after a period of time, quite the contrary is true. It is a common occurrence to receive a particular line within a hexagram twenty or more times, and another, never! In the example, the user has received the first line many times and the top line only once. By comparing the meanings of these lines within the context of the hexagram REFORM, it becomes immediately apparent that his mistakes and departures from correctness are rectified and reformed early, and he continues on his path with relative ease and success.

The "Hexagram Journal" in the back of the *Workbook* can be used to record your inquiries and answers. They should be dated and consistently recorded to aid you in cross-referencing. When you contemplate a certain hexagram or receive a particular changing line that you've received before (as noted in Column C), you may look up your original inquiry to recall how the situation resolved itself. This will lend clarity to subsequent divination and interpretation. Occasionally you should glance over the "Hexagram Journal" and take note of the questions of significance in your past. Contemplate the answers you've received. You will be amazed at their subtle complexities and remarkable accuracy.

If you keep a separate journal of your hexagrams, you may wish to develop other kinds of graphs. They might be based upon certain kinds or subjects of questions, focus on the frequency of various line positions, or you may align them with phases of the moon, biorhythms, astrological aspects, or whatever cycles interest you.

A final note: Take the time, now and then, to flip through the entire book and discover what patterns reveal themselves. Pick a hexagram at random and notice the way it has affected your life, and the way your life has affected its meaning. This is the spirit of approach taken by every individual who has ever written a commentary on *The Book of Change*. There is no reason why you should not write your own commentary with the same personal success. Allow this book to become your creation — and the next hexagram that you cast, its first breath.

This large, calligraphed character is the ideogram I *meaning "change."*
Some scholars believe it is derived from the early Chinese symbol
for lizard or chameleon while others feel that it is composed of the early
character for the sun placed over that of the moon.

C H A P T E R   I V

The Sixty-Four Hexagrams

1

CH'IEN

**ABOVE: CH'IEN
HEAVEN**

**BELOW: CH'IEN
HEAVEN**

**UPPER: CH'IEN
HEAVEN**

**LOWER: CH'IEN
HEAVEN**

RULING LINES

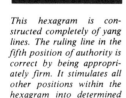

This hexagram is constructed completely of yang lines. The ruling line in the fifth position of authority is correct by being appropriately firm. It stimulates all other positions within the hexagram into determined and untiring strength.

CREATIVE POWER
(THE CREATIVE)

CREATIVE POWER is nothing less than the detonating device in the evolutionary bomb. The time is exceptional in terms of inspiration, energy, and will. It could be compared to the generative power of creation when the sperm enters and quickens the egg. The force of this time is the primal directive that propels us into our destinies regardless of what our reasoning or recalcitrant minds may think.

All activities will now center around your imperatives. You can now catapult yourself and others into great and significant activity. Direct this new strength wisely. Choose endeavors that will be useful and inspiring to all of humanity. Righteous and worthwhile goals will meet with sublime success.

In political or business affairs you will now be seen as the leader or governing force. Others will look to you for guidance and counsel. You have the opportunity to bring your personal desires into accord with the needs of society, thereby creating order and peace. You can create functions and laws and organize others with ease, and, in doing so, cause them to prosper and find happiness. With your example those around you will develop their higher senses. This is therefore a time of unparalleled significance.

Cast away from yourself all random interferences and unorganized trivia. You must use this time wisely and not squander the extraordinary *CREATIVE POWER* available to you on undirected activities. Everything you do will now lead you to still greater goals, so you should carefully conserve and direct your resources. Skillful timing is a great factor in this. Alert yourself to the intricate signals of the time by being constantly poised for action while maintaining strict discrimination and integrity. Know where your actions will lead. Know when *not* to act. Such masterful and sagacious awareness is truly the mark of a superior person.

Personal relationships will center around you. Your family or mate will look to you for leadership. Confidently take the initiative. At the same time, within the Self, all growth is accelerated. Develop inner strength by adhering to noble principles and far-reaching objectives. Ignore unimportant or irrelevant considerations. Success is imminent and will not be held off.

Without changing lines, *CREATIVE POWER* is a deeply significant omen. *The trigram,* CH'IEN, *creativity, is repeated above and below.* What you create now will be the basis and inspiration for what you experience next. As a result of any action you now take, your fate will be sealed. You may always trace back to the beginning, but there will never be an end to what you are about to set into motion.

Should all the lines be changing, the augury is indeed profound. Your character is thoroughly defined and balanced. You may now have a prominent and valuable effect upon the world.

TOP LINE

Your ambitions far exceed the possibilities of your *CREATIVE POWER*. If you pursue this dream you will lose touch with reality and lose contact with your community. You will no longer know how to behave appropriately and will ultimately regret your actions.

▶ FIFTH LINE

Whatever you choose to do is in accord with the cosmos. Your thinking is clearheaded. Because of this your influence is great and your milieu will look to you for inspiration.

FOURTH LINE

A time of choice is at hand. Because of an amplification in your *CREATIVE POWER* you must decide whether to enter the public eye and serve society, or whether to withdraw and work on your inner development. Follow your deepest intuition and you will not make a mistake.

THIRD LINE

A new world of *CREATIVE POWER* is opening to you. Others will become aware of this and attach themselves to you in hopes that they may use your gain in influence for their own aims. There is danger in this, for your energies may become distracted before they are stabilized. If you hold fiercely to your vision and integrity you will be protected.

SECOND LINE

Take note of a person who is active in the field of your interest. Although he may not be in a position of *CREATIVE POWER*, his conduct is above reproach and therefore he has significant influence. It would be to your advantage to align yourself with him.

BOTTOM LINE

The time is not ripe for action. You have all the *CREATIVE POWER* that you need to achieve your aim, but you must wait for the opportune moment. If necessary, you may direct activities from behind the scenes.

2

K'UN

**ABOVE: K'UN
EARTH**

**BELOW: K'UN
EARTH**

**UPPER: K'UN
EARTH**

**LOWER: K'UN
EARTH**

RULING LINES

This hexagram is contructed completely of yin lines. The ruler is in the second position of self-interest. It has all of the yielding attributes necessary for a NATURAL RESPONSE in human affairs.

NATURAL RESPONSE
(THE RECEPTIVE)

The yielding and responsive quality of nature is the focus of this time. Nature follows with sensitivity the demands of the seasons. It reproduces, adapts, and evolves itself appropriately; it heals itself when injured and deftly maintains a balanced economy. Nature is the responsive, yielding background for all events on earth. The power of this time lies in reacting with a *NATURAL RESPONSE* to the myriad things around you, a response in keeping with the laws of nature.

At this time you are dealing with realities rather than potentials. You can know only the situation around you but not the forces behind it. Therefore you should not act independently or try to lead others. If you do, you will lose the way and become confused. Because you are not connected to the forces at work in the situation, you need friends and helpers to accomplish your aims. If you can accept this you will find guidance. Once you respond naturally and allow yourself to be led, even the greatest goals can be attained.

By maintaining a pose of *NATURAL RESPONSE* even in the complex matters of business and politics, you can be assured that you are attuned to your own nature. At this time, such an attitude is of singular importance in your relations with worldly affairs. Through the help of friends and associates, you will be led into the best possible position. Above all, restrain the impulse to lead assertively in these situations.

You can begin to rely too much upon your own strength and forget that strength can be perilous when not directed properly. This time is a subtle study in nonaction as a way of attaining real meaning in your life. Relationships will be a test of this concept. It is important now to be particularly feeling and receptive of those dear to you. Allow them to take the initiative and assume the lead. Hold, at this time, to traditional values in the managing of interpersonal affairs and avoid aggressive attempts to get your way.

Within your Self, spend time alone in objective thought as you consider the direction of your life. Meditate upon the idea that everything on earth, good and evil, is supported by nature. Strive to broaden your attitudes and opinions and view the world with an open mind. Objectivity will keep your *NATURAL RESPONSE* pure while it gives you great stamina of character and inner calm in dealing with the outside world.

The trigram K'UN *is doubled. Receptivity above and below, within and without; it has no thrust but is completely receptive to all things.* In its unchanging form, *NATURAL RESPONSE* demands a more refined receptivity to your environment in general. Growth and change will be checked by subjective opinions. Open up your mind, expand your character to embrace the world. Then you will find guidance along the right path.

If all the lines are changing, it indicates that the longer you hold to your vision, the greater becomes your inner strength and personal power. You will reach your goal through endurance. This new situation will be a permanent one.

TOP LINE

An assertive and ambitious attempt is made to usurp power from an authority. A violent struggle will follow, resulting in injury to both parties.

FIFTH LINE

Do not display your potentials and virtues directly but allow them to permeate all of your affairs. Modesty and discretion about your inner worth yield the greatest good fortune.

FOURTH LINE

It is a difficult time, requiring caution. Develop an inner reserve and maintain a low profile. This can be done within the mainstream of society or in the strictest of solitude. Confrontations now will lead to antagonism or undesirable obligations.

THIRD LINE

Leave the pursuit of fame to others. Concentrate, instead, upon doing the best job possible. If you conceal your talents now, you will develop naturally, without interference. The time will come later for you to reveal yourself and your good works.

▶ SECOND LINE

Drop all artifice about what you are doing. Take your cue from nature: Become tolerant, straightforward, and self-evident. Strike an inner equilibrium at this time and success will come easily.

BOTTOM LINE

If you look carefully, you can see the very beginnings of decay entering the situation. Total deterioration is not far off. Make preparations now for the coming change.

3

CHUN

**ABOVE: K'AN
WATER**

**BELOW: CHEN
THUNDER**

**UPPER: KEN
MOUNTAIN**

**LOWER: K'UN
EARTH**

RULING LINES

The firm ruling line at the beginning works with the firm ruler in the fifth position of authority, bringing order to the remaining yielding lines.

DIFFICULT BEGINNINGS

The birth of every new venture begins in some confusion because we are entering the realm of the unknown. For this reason, a wrong step in the beginning can render the entire situation hopeless. Although this hexagram suggests nothing less than complete chaos, it ultimately presages a time of order and efficiency. Just as the tumultuous chaos of a thunderstorm brings a nurturing rain that allows life to flourish, so too in human affairs times of advanced organization are preceded by times of disorder. Success comes to those who can weather this storm while maintaining their principles.

DIFFICULT BEGINNINGS arise where there are a profusion of elements struggling to take form. You are facing such a situation. Because your new environment has yet to wholly materialize, much confusion surrounds any attempt to master it. Concentrate now on current problems, particularly in worldly affairs. The foundation upon which you will build all new ventures must be consolidated. In the meantime, do not attempt to break new ground. Your hands are full with myriad details that must be secured before you expand further. During *DIFFICULT BEGINNINGS* it is of utmost wisdom to hire able employees to assist you in your current business objectives. If you then continue to participate personally in your endeavors, you are promised supreme success.

This is a time when things are struggling to take form in the Self as well. *DIFFICULT BEGINNINGS* may mark an identity crisis, which could manifest as confusion, indecision, or new tastes and desires. Accept these changes in your Self without combating them. Meanwhile, look for examples of your desires so you will know where you are headed. Seek advice freely, but do not take it upon yourself to embark on new projects or untried ventures. Hold now to your own center and allow fate to manipulate external events. It will take all of the energy and powers of concentration you possess just to organize the profusion of information coming your way.

Confusion and disorder reign in personal relationships and there is little you can do about it. Remain calm during this new phase in your emotional life. Look outside the relationship for guidance. Whether professional or just friendly advice is sought, the very act of taking difficulties elsewhere will help you sort things out successfully. Remember, *DIFFICULT BEGINNINGS* is a phase of growth, and growing pains are in abundance. Yet, enduring this time with perseverance brings gratifying success.

When no lines are changing, the situation points to an obstacle that has not been surmounted. CHEN, *growth, in the lower trigram pushes upward into* K'AN, *difficulty, above.* This constant difficulty, present in the initial stages of movement, has not been resolved. Perhaps you do not recognize it as holding you back, or maybe you do not consider it a problem. Whatever the reason, the situation is blocked in regard to the object of your inquiry. Only by reorganizing your priorities will you transcend it.

TOP LINE

You have lost your perspective. You can no longer see your initial difficulties realistically, nor can you find your way out. This is disgraceful and will cause you much regret. It is best to begin again.

▶ FIFTH LINE

Although your position is one of authority within the situation, you have much left to achieve in the way of establishing yourself. Small efforts in this will bring good fortune. But beware: Do not attempt any large endeavor. It could easily end in disaster.

FOURTH LINE

With a little help, perhaps a connection you might exploit, you can attain your goals. Of course, you must admit that you lack sufficient power to act independently. If you hesitate over this, you will get nowhere.

THIRD LINE

You can sense the difficulties that lie ahead on your path. If you nevertheless plunge into the forest of obstacles without an experienced guide, you will surely lose your way. Such egotism and vanity brings unrelenting humiliation. A wiser man will alter his goals here.

SECOND LINE

Confusion and difficulty mount, and decisions become impossible. To allow yourself to accept help will create a hindering obligation. Therefore it is best to wait until the situation returns to normal before you continue in your pursuits.

▶ BOTTOM LINE

It seems that you have come across a confusing obstacle at the very beginning of your path. The best way to attract the helpers you will need is to maintain a devoted and humble attitude. Do not attempt to boldly push ahead unaided. However, do keep your goal in sight.

4

MENG

**ABOVE: KEN
MOUNTAIN**

**BELOW: K'AN
WATER**

**UPPER: K'UN
EARTH**

**LOWER: CHEN
THUNDER**

RULING LINES

*The firm line in the second
position of self-interest in-
structs the other yielding
lines. The ruling line in the
fifth position of authority
yields to the second line.
The firm line at the top is
severe in its wisdom.*

INEXPERIENCE
(YOUTHFUL FOLLY)

You are able to competently handle just about every facet of your life, except for the one facing you now. You have had enough experience in the twists and turns of your fate, and the inner workings of your nature, to dispense with most new situations that come your way, with the exception of this one. Your confusion over the difficulties and complexities of the coming event is not caused by ignorance, evil, or laziness, but rather by your complete *INEXPERIENCE* in dealing with such matters. Yet the time of *INEXPERIENCE* can bring you success because you are now forced to grow, to gain new insights, and to further develop your character.

First, know that you do not know what to do, then act accordingly. If you will not admit that there is something you must learn, you cannot be taught. And the time indicates that there is something, indeed, that you must discover. Look for an experienced teacher and seek his counsel and wisdom. Asking for help at this time is important in two ways. First, you will demonstrate to others that you are a willing and receptive pupil, thereby attracting information; and second, the process of requesting instruction will develop in you a useful predisposition toward the continued cultivation of your character. Life is a process of constant movement, change, and growth. There is no way to halt the process without ending it. This inevitable growth, without proper cultivation and guidance, can become distorted and lopsided.

Therefore, when seeking instruction, be certain that you are prepared to find, request, and use it properly. Approach a teacher who is clearly wiser in the matter causing you consternation and request advice with an open and humble attitude. If you cannot fully understand the advice you receive, or if it is not what you expected to hear, you may attribute this to your general *INEXPERIENCE*. If you knew the answer, you would not need to ask. You are dealing with a blind spot within your Self. Benefit from the experience of your teacher, for it is the only resource you have. And, above all, don't argue with your adviser. If you attempt to force him to justify his entire reasoning process you may alienate your teacher at a time when you desperately need help.

If you are an adviser of others, this hexagram will demonstrate to you, as well as the seeker, the proper attitude in such exchanges. If your pupil is not serious, is argumentative, or does not listen, do not waste your energies. Attend to other more important issues in your busy world.

K'AN, *the trigram of profound mystery, is struggling to attain meaning under the tremendous weight of stillness in the upper trigram,* KEN. In its static form, *INEXPERIENCE* suggests that a heretofore great mystery or misunderstood part of your nature must unfold and come forth before further progress can be made. With the proper questioning attitude and receptive frame of mind, success is indicated. In fact, once the mystery is unraveled you may experience what is known as "beginner's luck" in your next endeavor. However, don't let this go to your head.

TOP LINE

An inexperienced person may need to be punished for his mistakes in order to put him on the right path. Punishment is by no means an end in itself, but is useful only in preventing further transgressions and maintaining a progressive attitude.

▶ FIFTH LINE

An attitude of innocent acceptance in regard to seeking advice from others will be rewarded. Good fortune.

FOURTH LINE

Your fantasies and obsessions will consume you. Your attitude is unrealistic in regard to what is really going on in your life and therefore you cannot be instructed. You may ultimately be saved by experiencing fully the humiliation that follows.

THIRD LINE

You are in danger of throwing yourself away in a foolish attempt to be close to that which you fervently desire. Without strength of character and individuality you can accomplish nothing meaningful in life.

▶ SECOND LINE

The person in this position has indeed developed in himself a true appreciation of humanity in all of its folly and beauty. Such a person can lead others with wisdom, compassion, and inspiration, and attain all the success attributed to the great and wise historical leaders.

BOTTOM LINE

A little discipline is necessary here. There is not enough seriousness of attitude concerning the work to be done, and therefore the atmosphere is not conducive to proper growth. Yet, keep in mind that too many restrictions may lead to uncreative development. Apply just enough guidelines to keep things moving in the proper direction.

5

HSU

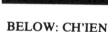

**ABOVE: K'AN
WATER**

**BELOW: CH'IEN
HEAVEN**

**UPPER: LI
FIRE**

**LOWER: TUI
LAKE**

RULING LINES

*The firm ruling line is in
the fifth position of authority in the upper trigram.
Yet it must wait for the
overly firm lower trigram to
change and stabilize.*

CALCULATED WAITING

A period of *CALCULATED WAITING* must pass before the cosmos can address itself to your needs. Many areas are undergoing significant change. Shifting powers are generating new ideas, animosities are appearing, alliances are forming, systems are breaking down, and collective causes are being organized. It is the eternal flux of change as manifested in human affairs.

That which you desire is caught in this change. In essence, it is a dangerous time, since the elements involved are not directly under your control. You may be facing some kind of threat or awaiting the outcome of a decision that could greatly affect you. If you worry about it you will grow inwardly confused and succumb to chaos and fear. You will waste valuable energy through agitation. When the time does come to act, your judgment may be impaired.

In order to attain your aim, you must wait to act until circumstances are in your favor. Inwardly bide your time and nourish and strengthen yourself for the future. Through careful observation attempt to see things without illusions or fears. Face the facts. If you are aware of your shortcomings and advantages, you will know what to do when the time comes. Ultimately you will meet with success.

In the meantime, the way that you conduct yourself outwardly is of great importance in the outcome of the situation. The time of *CALCULATED WAITING* will put your confidence to a test. It is now that you must make a show of confidence. Do not express your doubts about the past or the future. Indulge totally in the present. Keep your thoughts and words on a positive note and maintain an assured and cheerful attitude. In this way you will win the confidence of others and fortify your own certainty.

An external approach to inner development can be compared to yoga practices. By adopting certain physical postures of balance and discipline, a resonant chord is struck in the spirit. Such an alignment between the internal and the external creates a more sensitive consciousness, a certain enlightened awareness, and an overall healthy atmosphere.

In groups or relationships, all parties are involved in a situation that requires *CALCULATED* and good-natured *WAITING*. Those involved should realize that the situation is out of any one person's hands. Destiny is at work here. Any action would be a foolish overreaction, so nourish one another with cheerfulness and reassurance instead.

Creativity and strength in the lower trigram, CH'IEN, *are held in check by the profound mystery of* K'AN, *above. CALCULATED WAITING in its static form* implies that the area of your inquiry may be out of your grasp. What is involved in the attainment of your aim requires a more intricate understanding of the elements at work than you are capable of employing. Nothing can be done at this time, and the entire affair should be seen in the positive light of an important learning process.

TOP LINE

The time is complex. The waiting is over because the difficulties are upon you. There appears to be no way out of the situation. Yet help arrives if you recognize it. To know and graciously accept such unexpected and unfamiliar assistance will turn the entire situation toward the good.

▶ FIFTH LINE

Your difficulties are held in abeyance now and it is a good time to relax and gain perspective on the situation. While you enjoy your respite, keep in mind that there is still much to be done in the attainment of your goals.

FOURTH LINE

You are waiting in the very center of chaos. Any sort of confrontation with the problems that present themselves will only make things worse. Remove yourself immediately and unobtrusively from the situation.

THIRD LINE

Because of premature action on your part, inspired perhaps by anxiety, you will leave yourself open to attack. This situation is truly difficult because you are vulnerable. Only extreme caution will protect you.

SECOND LINE

What you propose to do will bring difficulties into your life. Furthermore, you could become a victim of gossip. If this occurs, don't try to defend yourself, as it will only lend weight to what is otherwise insubstantial. Success will eventually come.

BOTTOM LINE

Do not become agitated by your sense of an impending problem. Live your life as normally as possible and do nothing out of the ordinary. If there is a problem, it exists in the future. Acknowledging it now could diminish your strength.

6

SUNG

ABOVE: CH'IEN
HEAVEN

BELOW: K'AN
WATER

UPPER: SUN
WIND

LOWER: LI
FIRE

RULING LINES

The ruler in the fifth posi-
tion of authority is the only
line in its natural position.
It alone can arbitrate and
bring order. The rest are in
CONFLICT.

CONFLICT

In your heart you are certain that your proposed path is correct. You feel yourself to be in the right, and therefore you proceed with complete confidence. In fact, you are acting in accordance with your own nature and the dictates of the time. This path you have chosen, however, will lead you into a state of *CONFLICT*. Obstacles and opposition will rise up in front of you, and there is no way to circumvent them. Whether these are inner obstacles or external oppositions, they represent a formidable countermovement, since, from their point of view, they too are correct. This *CONFLICT* will cause you to stop and reconsider your original premise.

It would have been wise to cautiously weigh all of the possible difficulties and oppositions at the beginning of your endeavors. Such careful considerations are the only way to avoid debilitating *CONFLICT* which can bring your efforts to a standstill. As it is, you cannot engage in confrontation with your adversaries, for this would lead to misfortune. All such aggressive or cunning strategies will come to evil.

In questions of power or politics, it would be in your best interests to place the *CONFLICT* before an impartial authority who can make un unprejudiced decision. In this way you can bring discord to a halt before it becomes injurious. If you have planned an ambitious enterprise or have a goal of significance in mind, you would be advised to begin again at another time.

Business matters cannot be brought to fruition at this time. The competition is too great, and even carefully planned objectives will end in *CONFLICT*. You may meet with unfavorable reactions to ideas or products you thought to be totally acceptable. It would be best to hold back major changes or innovations until the time is more auspicious.

At a time when social unity is most important it is significantly lacking. There are misunderstandings brought about by basic philosophical differences and they cannot be overcome with forceful measures. Avoid controversial topics unless there is present a wise mediator who is trusted by all concerned. Social events of importance cannot be staged with any real success. If you can avoid them, do so.

Try to stay away from open confrontations in your personal relationships. It would be better to yield to those close to you rather than involve yourself in disagreements for which there is no ultimate resolution. A third person or disinterested party might now bring some insight to a *CONFLICT* of emotional interests. Above all, don't make any major decisions or demands based upon your own point of view. Although you may feel that your position is above reproach, you are dealing with only one side of the issue. Hold back and re-examine your original feelings.

In terms of inner development, your natural growth and patterns of interest have met with undeniable opposition. The time is one of spiritual maturing. Do not force the issue. A cautious yielding now leads to good fortune.

Firmness and creative purpose, CH'IEN, *in the upper trigram of cosmic ideals, meets with* K'AN, *danger and difficulty, in the more material world of human affairs, below.* CONFLICT *in its static form, suggests a significant breach with the object of your inquiry. You may be facing a major disillusionment in your life as you begin to realize that what you believed to be a universal truth is only your subjective view of the situation. You will have to reconsider your premise more realistically. The need for an inner adjustment yielding a more harmonious outlook is indicated.*

TOP LINE

If you engage now in forceful *CONFLICT*, it is possible you will emerge victorious. However, you will have created a situation of unending contest. Again and again, your position will be challenged. Such triumphs are ultimately meaningless.

▶ FIFTH LINE

Bring your *CONFLICT* before a powerful and just authority. If you are in the right, the situation will end in good fortune and success.

FOURTH LINE

You might see where you could improve your position by engaging in *CONFLICT* with a weaker element. The fact is, though, that you cannot gain inner satisfaction from such strategies. Returning to a sense of dignity and inner worth coupled with an acceptance of your fate will bring you peace of mind and good fortune.

THIRD LINE

Keep a low profile. Stick to established methods and traditional virtues. Do not put yourself in a position of prominence whatever you imagine to gain in prestige. Material possessions and status mean nothing now. Only your inner worth will be of value to you.

SECOND LINE

Your adversary is superior in strength. Do not allow your pride or sense of honor to draw you into open *CONFLICT*. Retreat and you will avoid a disastrous outcome for yourself and those close to you.

BOTTOM LINE

Your position is such that you must avoid any *CONFLICT* or terminate it quickly. Don't try to bring things to a decision or engage yourself in a dispute. You may feel a little victimized, but in the end all goes well.

7

SHIH

**ABOVE: K'UN
EARTH**

**BELOW: K'AN
WATER**

**UPPER: K'UN
EARTH**

**LOWER: CHEN
THUNDER**

RULING LINES

The ruler in the upper trigram of cosmic ideals yields to the strong ruler in the lower trigram of human affairs. These worldly affairs are the COLLECTIVE FORCE that controls the hexagram.

COLLECTIVE FORCE
(THE ARMY)

When an object has mass, it is said to have gravity. The denser its mass, the greater the dynamic force of its gravity. Within our own solar system, a large planet like Jupiter attracts with a powerful force nearly three times that of our smaller earth. This forceful law of gravity and masses, effective throughout all the cosmos, is significantly effective among large masses of people as they focus the awesome strength of their *COLLECTIVE FORCE.*

The time of *COLLECTIVE FORCE* requires great discipline, organization, and righteous aims. Those in authority must have confidence in you, and you must gain support from the people around you as you continue in your endeavors. This energy of mass support can be tapped now if you are communicating effectively and if your goals are in accordance with the sentiments of society.

Supportiveness and generosity toward others can accomplish the difficult task of uniting the masses. Originally titled *The Army,* this hexagram points to the necessity of organizing and experiencing this *COLLECTIVE FORCE,* although it warns against using it for dangerous warlike purposes unless there exists no other alternative. Clearly, a strong leader is required for this task, while the time is especially auspicious for those in positions of authority. People can now be most effectively led through education, generosity, and leniency. At the same time they must be inspired by a noble vision and impressed by firm principles.

Any venture now requires a strong inner conviction of your correctness. You must assume that you are acting with the *COLLECTIVE FORCE* behind you. If you feel unconnected from your society then you must make it a point to find and experience this powerful resource inherent in humanity. Naturally, this takes exceptional awareness and determination, but the strong man who achieves this will meet with good fortune.

Be generous now and accommodating in your personal relationships. Try to see your roles together in the context of all of humanity. A more philosophical point of view can do wonders at this time, whereas a focus upon the more eccentric aspects of your relationships can lead you astray. Hold together with your loved ones and attempt to overcome any difficulties with the gravity of your *COLLECTIVE FORCE.* This force is the basis of organization and continuity, whether in a solar system or in a love affair.

Ultimately, in matters of your external relationships you must always return to the center of the Self for orientation and processing. This is a fine time to broaden your ideals to encompass larger goals — the goals of all of mankind. This will eventually strengthen your ability to call upon the *COLLECTIVE FORCE* in dangerous times. Concurrently, you will also hear the call of this force as it grows, changes, and informs.

The *COLLECTIVE FORCE* in its static form becomes a plateau in your development. Before you can continue to progress, you must acquaint yourself with the goals of humanity, for they, in fact, affect your own aims. *The profound and mysterious* K'AN, *in the lower trigram of human affairs, is affecting the course of cosmic affairs in the upper trigram,* K'UN, *responsiveness and receptivity.* Be open now and generous toward the feelings and needs of others. In this way you align yourself with humanity and increase your energies and resources.

TOP LINE

Your aim is achieved. When settling into the new situation be certain to align your proprieties to worthwhile values. Inferior persons and ideas should be assigned to their proper places. Do not give them a voice in your affairs.

▶ FIFTH LINE

Rely on an experienced person to lead the way in correcting the situation. He must be moderate in his behavior and not overreactive, for this would lead to misfortune. Inexperienced and enthusiastic persons are now inappropriate for the job of deliberate and controlled leadership.

FOURTH LINE

The obstacles ahead are insurmountable. Struggling against them is useless. Therefore the intelligent maneuver is retreat.

THIRD LINE

There is an absence of vision and leadership. Whether it is a matter of divergent goals or whether the acting leader is simply inept, the result is the same: misfortune.

▶ SECOND LINE

You are in an excellent position to communicate with others. Because this situation is so well disposed you will meet with good fortune and win recognition from your superiors.

BOTTOM LINE

Before you take action, be certain that what you propose is worthwhile, for otherwise you cannot sustain yourself. Be sure as well that you are organized. Without order, your affairs will end in chaos and misfortune. Discipline is the key here.

8

PI

**ABOVE: K'AN
WATER**

**BELOW: K'UN
EARTH**

**UPPER: KEN
MOUNTAIN**

**LOWER: K'UN
EARTH**

RULING LINES

▶

*The firm ruling line in the
position of authority bonds
all yielding lines together
into UNITY.*

UNITY
(HOLDING TOGETHER)

As a part of civilization, man is also a product of civilization. He shares with the other members certain intrinsic experiences peculiar to his community. This creates in turn a bond of language, order, and tradition, which are the foundations for the progress and evolution of both the community and the individual. His relationships to his immediate society may be many and varied. He may feel rebellious or conservative, apathetic or highly conscious, he may be lauded or incarcerated. Whatever his circumstances, he is inexorably a member of the social order.

You are surrounded at this time by an awareness of your society. Whatever your inquiry, you must first address yourself to this issue. It is of great importance that the need for creating *UNITY* is recognized. The individual human spirit is nourished by a sense of connectedness to the whole of human awareness. This perspective will enhance your sense of direction. You will be able to glimpse yourself as a part of a whole, which will both amplify your individuality and annihilate it. Do not fear this, for it will not diminish your self-awareness but rather spotlight it against a more profound background.

The Chinese text urges that on some level *UNITY* takes place when opportunities first arise. These are important experiences in the development of character. If you continue to ignore these opportunities you are more and more excluded from your community and rendered ineffectual in terms of influence: Not only will you have little to say, but also very few will be listening. Whether you interpret this as voting in an upcoming election, joining a public-minded organization, attending or supporting a cultural event, or simply adopting a more responsible attitude about your neighborhood, now is the time to act. In interpersonal affairs, look both within the relationship for *UNITY* and beyond it for its meaning within society. There is a time for exclusivity and a time for social *UNITY* and productivity.

This hexagram has another equally important aspect: It may be that an opportunity has presented itself for you to be the leader of *UNITY*, to gather the members of society together, to influence them, to advance them. Keep in mind that this position requires great responsibility, virtue, and a true sense of purpose. If you are not up to such a role and yet endeavor to undertake it, you will create only chaos and confusion.

So important does the *I Ching* regard this role that it suggests that one who feels such a calling consult the oracle once again to determine the state of his character, the integrity of his motives, and his harmony with the cosmos.

The receptive trigram K'UN *is striving upward to make a meaningful connection with* K'AN, *the profound.* Receiving *UNITY in its static form suggests that without strong social connections you may indeed become an island isolated in the sea of your own illusions. Make an attempt to embrace the opinions and perceptions of others, if only for a moment. Cross the sea and explore new frontiers of ideas.*

TOP LINE

The moment for *UNITY* has passed. Right from the beginning something was amiss and all attempts toward union inspired failure. Examine the situation to determine the extent of your error.

▶ FIFTH LINE

You can trust fate at this time to bring you together with those who would further you. There is a natural attraction at work here. The atmosphere is liberal, and much can be accomplished. The time is auspicious, indeed.

FOURTH LINE

You are in close contact with the center of your community. This may refer to the leader or ruler. Show your support openly, but do not forget who you are or lose yourself in your allegiances.

THIRD LINE

The people in the environment of your inquiry are not right for you at this time. Avoid too intimate an association with the group while maintaining an outward sociability. Appearing committed to these people could darken your reputation later on.

SECOND LINE

Trust your inner mind, maintain your integrity, and follow the demands of your convictions. You will be sought after by others. If you chase after the approval of others, you will lose your dignity.

BOTTOM LINE

An honest, unaffected attitude is an excellent basis for forming associations. With such an attitude you can be confident that others will be attracted to you. Unexpected good luck is indicated here.

9

HSIAO CH'U

ABOVE: SUN
WIND

BELOW: CH'IEN
HEAVEN

UPPER: LI
FIRE

LOWER: TUI
LAKE

RULING LINES

The only yielding, therefore significant, line in the fourth position of social concerns yields to the strong ruler in the fifth position of authority. Yet the fourth line restrains all the others.

RESTRAINED
(THE TAMING POWER OF THE SMALL)

It is as if your strong impulses, good intentions, and serious plans were held in check by some unknown external detail.. With some frustration, you can see all of the necessary elements in the attainment of your goals; yet nothing fits together the way it must. In every way you try, you are *RESTRAINED* from taking significant action. The ancient Chinese described this hexagram as "Dense clouds, no rain," a singularly unfulfilling situation. However, there is some promise of mild success through small, gentle improvements. Grand schemes are out of the question.

You may now only exercise the most brief and gentle of influences over others. The powers of the status quo are formidable and not to be tampered with. Your best plan, during these *RESTRAINED* times, is to stay close to the situation you wish to affect. Use the forces of friendly persuasion to maintain what influence you have and to keep the situation from running away without you. Quell any impulses to take aggressive measures.

As you may have already discovered, this is a poor time for new business ventures. Even though prospects may look promising, it will be best to wait for the signs of a sure success. In the meantime, attend to the details of the business at hand. Improve the appearance or format of your product but do not attempt to introduce a sweeping modification. In this way you will still be around when the situation is no longer *RESTRAINED*.

It is going to take great skillfulness to achieve a successful outcome in personal relationships. You have no control over the affair whatsoever, and arguments or ultimatums can accomplish nothing. Your choice is either to acquiesce and wait out the *RESTRAINED* atmosphere in a friendly manner, or to depart from the relationship altogether.

However, rather than anguishing over these conflicts, your time would be best spent in improving your image. Exercise restraint over your opinions and belief systems and put your energies into your effect upon others. Try to anticipate what facet of your personality you can display to give you the greatest advantage over your environment. This then becomes your major asset and device of persuasion during times when significant influence is unlikely. There is, nevertheless, a prospect for ultimate success if you can restrain yourself until the situation can accommodate your plan.

CH'IEN, *strength, is restrained in the lower trigram of human affairs and can create only small and gentle effects as shown by* SUN, *in the higher realms.* The hexagram *RESTRAINED*, in its unchanging form, suggests that the object of your inquiry is blocked by a small yet permanent influence. Nothing can be done externally. Salvation, if it exists, lies in work on the Self. Refine your impulses and desires.

TOP LINE

You have won the battle. Rest and consolidate your position now and restrain yourself from going after the entire war. Caution: Adversity is on the rise. If you attempt to push ahead, you will meet with misfortune.

▶ FIFTH LINE

Through a co-operative and loyal relationship with another, you increase your resources mutually. In this way you can accomplish your aim.

FOURTH LINE

If you are honest and sincere and influence others with the correct advice, you can avoid existing and terrible dangers. Fear and anxiety will give way only to truth. Then no error will be made.

THIRD LINE

The opposition appears minor and advance seems possible. Yet the situation is not in your control. If you insist upon forging ahead confidently you will be defeated by no end of annoyances. This has a most undignified appearance.

SECOND LINE

Athough you might like to take action, it would be wise to re-evaluate the situation and study the examples of others who have come before you. The time suggests that a retreat leads to good fortune.

BOTTOM LINE

In forcing your way, you meet with obstacles. It is best to hold back to a position where you have the choice of advance or retreat. Then you may concern yourself with the true nature of the situation and react accordingly.

10

LU

**ABOVE: CH'IEN
HEAVEN**

**BELOW: TUI
LAKE**

**UPPER: SUN
WIND**

**LOWER: LI
FIRE**

RULING LINES

The firm correct ruler in the fifth position of authority recognizes the bold advances made by the yielding line in the third position of personal goals and ambitions. The ruler conducts itself appropriately because of its correctness.

CONDUCT

This can be a brilliant and inspiring time. It can also be a time of danger. Everything depends upon the way that you *CONDUCT* yourself. The best possibility for progress and success comes through your sense of dignity and composure. Disorder and chaos cannot touch you if you behave with propriety and good manners.

Pay special attention to your *CONDUCT* in social affairs. When in doubt, maintain your dignity. You may suddenly come face to face with the necessity of becoming truly discriminating in your choice of acquaintances. The process of social readjustment is in the air. Some are climbing. Some are falling. It's a natural occurrence. No one will be hurt. These cycles of balance and discrimination, based upon the inner worth of the individuals involved, will bring order and progress to society.

When you are dealing with matters of business, you must *CONDUCT* yourself with great care and dignity. Persons below you may make a bold approach or perhaps an unexpected advance. Base your reactions upon the inner worth of these people, and your authority will not be challenged. In this way you can avoid incompetence caused by prejudice or eccentric whims on your part. If you, yourself, are embarking on ambitious endeavors you may find success in your pursuits. Stick to traditional behavior patterns, however, in spite of your daring.

The time is truly difficult in personal relationships. Consider now the goals and desires of those close to you. If there are misunderstandings or confusion, maintain your composure. Good fortune comes through conducting yourself with thoughtfulness and courtesy. If you or your loved ones are contemplating a wild emotional move, whatever the circumstances, it is now ill advised. By bringing a little dignity into your relationships you can create an atmosphere for emotional growth and progress.

In terms of general attitude, maintain your composure at all costs. The way that you *CONDUCT* yourself now will determine the outcome of any external situation. You can avoid poor health brought about by stress if you adopt a good-natured outlook. Above all, use this time to develop a sense of your own Self worth. Take note of your outstanding character traits and continue to cultivate your inner growth in the direction of these worthier virtues.

There exists a difference in the interests of the component trigrams. CH'IEN, firmness and creative strength, above, is concerned with cosmic ideals, while TUI, satisfaction and openness, below, is concerned with the details of human affairs. When CONDUCT is received without changing lines there arises some question of your values. You may be overly opinionated and lost in decorum in regard to the object of your inquiry, or you may be altogether too indiscriminate in what you allow to influence you. In order to make progress you must now bring some equilibrium into your tastes.

TOP LINE

Take a long look at what your *CONDUCT* in the situation has achieved thus far. If you are on the right path you will know by the good it has produced. It is time for a reevaluation of your goals. By examining the past you may now get a glimpse of the future.

▶ FIFTH LINE

What you propose to do is dangerous, yet your awareness of such danger will give you the strength to succeed. The time requires a firm commitment to your endeavor. If you do not have a real commitment in your heart you should re-examine your path.

FOURTH LINE

You can now undertake even dangerous endeavors if you proceed with great caution.

THIRD LINE

You are not suited for the ambitiousness of your goals. Your powers are not adequate. Willfulness on your part could end in disaster. Such *CONDUCT* is only for someone willing to throw himself away for a superior.

SECOND LINE

Maintain an ambiance of modesty and moderation. Do not harbor expectations or demands. Do not get involved with the dreams of others or hold overly ambitious goals. In this way you will meet with good fortune.

BOTTOM LINE

Use your most basic values of *CONDUCT* in advancing toward your aim. Do not try to use others beyond maintaining friendly relations. Do not become obligated to others in your endeavors. Your position is low. Simplicity in your behavior will prevent mistakes and allow you to progress.

11

T'AI

**ABOVE: K'UN
EARTH**

**BELOW: CH'IEN
HEAVEN**

**UPPER: CHEN
THUNDER**

**LOWER: TUI
LAKE**

RULING LINES

The firm ruler in the center of the lower trigram of human affairs meets with great receptivity the yielding ruler in the center of the upper trigram of cosmic ideals. The result is co-operation and progress.

PROSPERING
(PEACE)

The time resembles the exciting beginning of spring, when the cosmic forces are in inspired harmony. There presently exist the ideal conditions for new awakenings, healthy growth, and progressive plans. It is a totally co-operative environmental setting that leads to the flowering and *PROSPERING* of what is now aroused.

When spring comes to any situation, the superior man uses his awareness of this cosmic signal to cultivate the fertile ground presented. He separates, regulates, controls, and limits the rich beginnings so as to shape the future and organize his life. It is possible now for strong and good ideas to advance the situation while reforming the inferior and degenerating elements of the past.

Your interactions with others can be exceptionally fruitful. If you have avoided social situations in the recent past, you should now feel confident about making contacts. There is an end to animosities as mistrust and factionalism depart and good feelings prevail. The exchange of good influences can create the structure for a *PROSPERING* social environment.

Many things will become possible as the wisest leaders move with ease into ruling positions. Such men are so magnanimous and progressive that even the most evil elements change for the better. Because of the correct and harmonious nature of the cosmic forces present, it is an excellent time for making useful laws and developing advanced systems of order. Success then comes easily to all the individual members of a *PROSPERING* government.

Business situations will experience a most direct benefit from this fortunate time. Use the *PROSPERING* environment to bring organization to your endeavors. The current clarity, like the beginning of spring, lends itself to the initiation of systems that will continue to benefit, even in hard times. Service organizations and people who work with others will make particularly significant gains at this time.

Within the Self, the focus is on inner harmony. The outward aspect of your nature will reflect a certain peace that comes from the *PROSPERING* of the spirit. There exists now a harmonious accord between your instincts and the cosmic forces. Your most innocent actions will benefit yourself and others. Your personal relationships may remain the same externally, but your attitude will significantly improve. At the same time, your physical well-being will benefit. You will feel a new strength developing as weakening and degenerative elements depart. Generally, this time brings a peace of mind, which alone creates an all-encompassing atmosphere for success and prosperity.

The trigrams are well disposed toward each other. K'UN, *responsiveness, in the upper trigram of cosmic ideals is totally receptive and lends insight to* CH'IEN, *creative strength, in the lower trigram of human interests.* Without changing lines, *PROSPERING* reflects the successful, if benign, environment of harmonious accord. In its static form it is an unusually auspicious omen requiring, nonetheless, a sense of responsibility toward others. To use this time to its best advantage, analyze the harmony present, seek to penetrate the nature of accord, and recognize the signs of unobstructed communication between heaven and earth.

TOP LINE

A decline has begun. It is of the external world, and nothing can be done to hold it back. Such attempts will bring you humiliation. Instead, devote your time to strengthening your ties with those close to you.

▶ FIFTH LINE

You can achieve your aim and realize great good fortune by remaining impartial in your behavior. Humility and modesty will allow you to communicate with the sentiments of your followers in mind. You will then be supported in your endeavors.

FOURTH LINE

The important thing now is that you are sincerely united and communicating with people who are your superiors. Pay no thought to ultimate rewards but maintain a steady course toward your aim. Use the help of others, if offered.

THIRD LINE

You may see a decision approaching, for the laws of change are eternally active. Any difficulties can be endured with an inner faith in your own strength and perseverance. Meanwhile, enjoy fully the present.

▶ SECOND LINE

During *PROSPERING* times it is important to hold to worthy attitudes and behavior in order to achieve your aim. You now have a responsibility to undertake difficult tasks, to be tolerant of all people, and to maintain far-reaching visions. Avoid getting involved in current factions and special-interest groups.

BOTTOM LINE

Actions that you might now take, particularly those actions that are connected to the welfare of others, will meet with good fortune. You will attract others and find co-operation among those who have goals similar to your own.

12

P'I

**ABOVE: CH'IEN
HEAVEN**

**BELOW: K'UN
EARTH**

**UPPER: SUN
WIND**

**LOWER: KEN
MOUNTAIN**

RULING LINES

The lower trigram of human affairs is totally yielding and inferior, while the correct ruler in the fifth position of authority is surrounded and isolated by incorrect lines. There is no communication.

STAGNATION

The forces in nature are in a state of perfect and undiscriminating impasse. There is no responsive action between things, and nothing productive can be accomplished. The natural order that nourishes and fosters all things is disjointed and disunited. The lines of communication are down. Because of this there is no understanding of what is needed, and growth cannot continue. When growth stops, *STAGNATION* begins.

Any useful insights or ideas you may have will be met with apathy or rejection. The atmosphere of your environment is unreceptive even to altruistic and unselfish energies on your part. The problem is not in your motives. Whether you seek to turn a quick profit, or volunteer the whole of your resources to a worthwhile social cause, you can accomplish nothing. *STAGNATION* is a reservoir of arbitrary and absurd misunderstandings.

STAGNATION produces an ambiance of decay and decadence. Inferior persons and ideas can rise to positions of great influence. The political and social environment can become corrupt indeed, and there is little a person of principle can do to turn the tide of events. Leaders are not in touch with the people whom they lead, and social systems become irrelevant. The people become lost in a labyrinth of discordant purpose and are filled with mistrust. Things come to a standstill and people, therefore, cannot be helped.

Your social life may ebb due to a lack of meaningful discourse. Artistic endeavors, touted as brilliant or *avant-garde,* will seem to you inferior and lacking in inspiration. Or perhaps truly inspired works will be completely overlooked by your milieu. Do not doubt your inner vision or ethics. *STAGNATION* is a difficult time and, in reality, there is nothing you can do. If you participate in public activities you will resonate with the atmosphere and become stagnant yourself. You must, at all costs, avoid the confusion that comes when there is absolute discord in the cosmos. Withdraw.

Do not attempt to influence others, for this is not possible. Do not compromise your principles or alter your standards, for there is no end to the chaos and nothing reasonable can be resolved. You will be pulled farther and farther into multifarious disorder. Do not be tempted by promises of rewards or extravagant remunerations in return for your participation in a stagnant situation. The cost to your integrity will be too dear. Instead, you must conceal your convictions and remove yourself from any situation that will cause you conflict until the time of *STAGNATION* passes.

Relationships will be difficult at this time and you may, in fact, be adrift in a sea of misunderstandings and miscommunications. Hold courageously and unobtrusively to your values and inner confidence, for these times will certainly pass. This is true in matters of health as well. Self-reliance will see you through.

The trigrams at work in this hexagram are profoundly juxtaposed. CH'IEN, *creativity, is moving up and away from* K'UN, *receptivity. Useful and important communications cannot occur. Because of the strong counterforces at work here,* STAGNATION *without changing lines indicates that the object of your inquiry may not be in harmony with the larger direction of your life at any time.*

TOP LINE

The opportunity to change a situation from *STAGNATION* to progress is at hand. It will not happen of its own accord. A strong and continuing sense of purpose is necessary to achieve and maintain the greatest possible heights of success.

▶ FIFTH LINE

A sweeping change for the better is indicated. Things can improve and progress. Yet this is the very time to feel cautious and reserved. With such an attitude your success is doubly insured and a strong foundation is established for the new times.

FOURTH LINE

It is possible to change the entire situation to one of progress and order. If you sincerely hear a calling to the task and are in harmony with the cosmos, you and your associates will benefit. If you simply appoint yourself to the position of leader, confusion could result.

THIRD LINE

Because of questionable methods and motives used to attain your position, your plans will not come to fruition. There is some shame in this, but therefore improvement.

SECOND LINE

It is better to quietly accept *STAGNATION* than to attempt to influence the leaders and willing victims of the situation. By remaining apart, you will not corrupt your principles. Success is indicated.

BOTTOM LINE

If it is not possible to change or influence the current environment while preserving the principles that have formed your character, then withdraw completely. Success will come to you in a more profound sense than could be realized from a compromising situation. Important associates may leave with you. Good fortune.

13

T'UNG JEN

**ABOVE: CH'IEN
HEAVEN**

**BELOW: LI
FIRE**

**UPPER: CH'IEN
HEAVEN**

**LOWER: SUN
WIND**

RULING LINES

The yielding ruler in the second position of self-interest is aligned to the strong ruler in the fifth position of authority. Both are correct. All lines benefit.

COMMUNITY
(FELLOWSHIP WITH MEN)

Society functions at its very best when each member finds security in his place within the social structure. When all members can be gainfully employed, yet have individual initiative, when they can excel in their own craft, and in doing so contribute to the overall goals of society, then there exists harmony and a sense of *COMMUNITY*. When the members have an interest in the continuity of their *COMMUNITY*, great deeds can be accomplished. This is because the many work for the one.

Whether you live and function in the midst of society, or whether you have created for yourself a life outside of the mainstream, you are affected by all social considerations: by the traditions of the *COMMUNITY*, by its economy, and by its laws. In the overall scope of evolution, the desirability of becoming self-sufficient and independent and living outside of society is as unfeasible as it is archaic. The benefits of isolation at this time are questionable. Therefore you must now evaluate your life and your goals in the light of the needs of your *COMMUNITY*.

It may be that you are in a position to help organize your *COMMUNITY*. This role requires great strength of character and the complete elimination of all self-serving motives. The time is beneficial for the attainment of social aims, yet this benefit will be lost with selfish interests and separatist endeavors. When organizing others, it is necessary to assign each member his place within the group. Without order, rank, and system the gathering would become a mere mingling and little could be accomplished. Make intelligent, thoughtful discriminations of the various talents of others. Put each person where he will most effectively function and at the same time find satisfaction in his work. Do not assume that this will just "happen." If the needs of humanity are to be met there must be a superior leader to instill social order. If you are, instead, a member of the *COMMUNITY*, maintain a consistent and principled attitude about your craft or job. Your own promised success at this time will serve as an example and thereby will benefit others as well as yourself.

Generally, it is a fine time for new endeavors. The forces present in this hexagram favor the creation of structures, mechanisms, and healthy disciplines necessary for the unified attainment of ambitious deeds, particularly when these deeds are aligned to and serve the needs of your fellow man.

The family is a microcosm of the *COMMUNITY*, and here too you should concern yourself with the direction of your personal goals. Are they consonant with the well-being of those dear to you? This is not the time to strike out as an individual.

The static hexagram indicates that the companionship of others satisfies your deepest needs. *The lower trigram, LI, attachment, moves up into the realm of creative strength,* CH'IEN. The result of a commitment to your *COMMUNITY* will develop in you a strong moral fiber. This is the next necessary step in the growth of your character.

TOP LINE

The unity and fellowship that are possible in this position are not significant in terms of universal needs. However, joining with others, even in a small way, is not a mistake.

▶ FIFTH LINE

The difficulties and obstacles within the situation cause you much sorrow. If you openly express your distress you will find that you generate similar expressions from your fellow man. Together you can overcome the difficult time and there will be much joy in your newfound unity.

FOURTH LINE

Your obsession with the attainment of your personal goals will ultimately cut you off from others. The more you pursue your dream, the farther you drift from your *COMMUNITY*. In time, your loneliness will bring you to your senses. Good fortune.

THIRD LINE

There is a possibility that those involved in the situation have selfish interests and divergent goals. This is unfortunate, because the ensuing mistrust of each for the other will grind events to a halt. Unless goals are realigned, no progress can be made and nothing will come of the situation.

▶ SECOND LINE

There is a tendency toward elitism and exclusivity. This creates limitations for everyone in society. Such a situation of egotism and selfish interests will bring regret.

BOTTOM LINE

The times are such that a group of people all share the same needs. They can come together openly with the same goals in mind. This is the beginning of a fellowship. Until the interests of the individuals become divergent all will go well.

14

TA YU

**ABOVE: LI
FIRE**

**BELOW: CH'IEN
HEAVEN**

**UPPER: TUI
LAKE**

**LOWER: CH'IEN
HEAVEN**

RULING LINES

▶

The ruler in the fifth position of authority is respected for its receptive nature. Because it poses no threat, it is granted SOVEREIGNTY by all the other firm lines.

SOVEREIGNTY
(POSSESSION IN GREAT MEASURE)

Because of a stroke of good fortune you will meet with supreme success. At few times do you possess more. Seldom are you able to receive as much. Your position has become one of authority within the situation of your inquiry, yet you continue in an attitude of unassuming modesty. With such an attitude you pose no threat to those around you and they, therefore, loyally align themselves to your authority. Thus you are granted SOVEREIGNTY. This power should be controlled with moderation and modesty, leading you into a state of great progress and potential.

You are in the spotlight, exposed to the view of both those you lead and those above you: Therefore proper behavior is necessary in order to continue in your accomplishments. Keep your ego in check. Never forget that things move to change at the first sign of imbalance. Your values must be realistic. Examine yourself for signs of pride, which are inappropriate to someone in a position of SOVEREIGNTY. You must now fight to suppress evil in yourself and in the general situation by adhering to things that are good. Your strength comes through your alignment to the cosmic order in which good and evil find their proper places.*

Your dealings in worldly affairs will meet with success. This might mean material wealth. Even your superiors wisely acquiesce to your SOVEREIGNTY as you continue in your progress. With an unselfish attitude and goals that place emphasis on cultural achievements, you will realize the greatest rewards.

In social matters, even the strongest members of your community will defer to you. With gentleness and goodness you will win their hearts. Through compassion — that is, identifying with others and finding the possibilities of their weaknesses within yourself — you move them to loyalty and gain their obedience. If you are an artist, your creative inspirations are now relevant to your culture, and you will meet with great success. Furthermore, your personal relationships, although lacking in passion, are well ordered. Here too you hold the position of SOVEREIGNTY and, if you are kind and unselfish, your relationships will flower.

Within the Self, SOVEREIGNTY may be a burden as well as a blessing. When experiencing material successes, you most easily fall victim to such vices as pride, greed, and immodesty. You must now make special efforts to curb any attitudes that will lead to humiliation and thus weaken your character. Instead, focus your attention upon those qualities in yourself that enhance your goodness.

CH'IEN, *strength, in the lower trigram of human affairs relies upon* LI, *clarity, in the upper trigram of cosmic ideals, to provide proper direction.* In its static form, the hexagram SOVEREIGNTY demands a firm adherence to your principles regarding the object of your inquiry. There should be no dogma or pretension in your words, ideas, and convictions. Absolute clarity of mind combined with strength of character will give you the integrity necessary to accomplish your aim and continue past this time. If SOVEREIGNTY becomes institutionalized, it loses direction.

---

* Lao Tzu, a sixth-century B.C. Chinese philosopher, says of this idea:

> The best rulers are those whose existence is merely known by the people.
> The next best are those who are loved and praised.
> The next are those who are feared.
> And the next are those who are despised.
> It is only when one does not have enough faith in others that others will have no faith in him.
> The great rulers value their words highly.
> They accomplish their task; they complete their work.
> Nevertheless, their people say that they simply follow Nature.

TOP LINE

Here lies the potential for great blessings and good fortune. Know how to keep things in balance; be devoted in your endeavors and openly appreciative to those who help you. In this way you might expect supreme success.

▶ FIFTH LINE

Those whom you may influence are attracted to you through the bond of sincerity. Thus a truthful relationship exists. If you are overly familiar, however, attitudes may become too casual to get things accomplished. A dignified approach brings good fortune.

FOURTH LINE

Quell your pride and envy and do not attempt to compete with others or emulate those in power. Give your full attention to the business at hand and you will avoid mistakes.

THIRD LINE

A superior-minded person will place his talents or resources at the disposal of his leader or his community. Through this type of open generosity he is benefited, for he is loyally supported in turn. A lesser man cannot do this.

SECOND LINE

You not only have tremendous resources to work with, but you also possess the wherewithall to coordinate these assets and make them work for you. Such ingenuity will allow you to fearlessly attempt ambitious endeavors.

BOTTOM LINE

Although you possess a great deal, you have not yet been challenged in your position. Therefore you have made no mistakes. Keep in mind that the situation is at its beginning and difficulties may lie on the road ahead. With forewarned awareness you can remain blameless.

15

CH'IEN

ABOVE: K'UN EARTH

BELOW: KEN MOUNTAIN

UPPER: CHEN THUNDER

LOWER: K'AN WATER

RULING LINES

The only firm line in the hexagram stands in the third position and is correct. It moderately rules in the interest of human affairs from the top line of the lower trigram.

MODERATION
(MODESTY)

The predominant forces in the cosmos at this time are in the process of balancing extremes and harmonizing interests. This tendency toward equilibrium and *MODERATION* is a natural urge in the universe. In the terrain of the earth, pinnacles are in the process of wearing down and valleys are filling up. Extreme poles magnetize and attract their opposites, thus neutralizing and moderating themselves. Nature balances itself with plagues, droughts, and cycles of overabundance, and human nature strives toward *MODERATION* in its tendency to reduce the excesses of the overpowerful and to augment the needs of those who are desperately wanting.

Worldly matters can now be brought to success through *MODERATION*. Leaders should strive to firmly carry their objectives through to completion, not with a show of extraordinary force but with the continuing sincerity that springs from their true natures. Confucius says of this idea, "When a man enters public life he does not change from what he was in private life. How unflinching is his strength!" The self-evident, self-actualizing demonstration of purpose is the mark of great leaders acting with *MODERATION*.

In social relationships, avoid extremes. People who are overly intelligent or overly ignorant tend to extremes in their behavior and attitudes. You should now concentrate upon establishing a harmonious equilibrium with your fellow man and bring *MODERATION* and order to social institutions. This not only means avoiding radicalism and ostentatious values but also tolerating weaknesses and inferior elements. "Everything in moderation" means just that.

This is a good time to bring some equilibrium to your more personal relationships. Examine your deepest feelings and see if you are harboring any extremes in your expectations or selfish desires in your motivations. Try to moderate any unrealistic ideals.

Your inner development now requires a modest and sincere attitude. Do not indulge in extremes of any sort, and instead strive for *MODERATION* in all you do.* It must be understood that acting with *MODERATION* means not only limiting the obvious excesses, but also exposing yourself to new areas of experience. Through *MODERATION* you can now gain some real control over your destiny. In this way you use the balancing tendency of the current forces to center yourself. This inner equilibrium aligns you with the *tao*, thus bringing you into harmony with forces that can work for you.

CH'IEN, *firmness, in the upper trigram of cosmic ideals is full of its own strength while the mountainous* KEN, *stillness, is immovable in the lower trigram of human affairs. Each is an extreme, yet the existence of each moderates the other.* Without changing lines, the hexagram *MODERATION* reflects a need for temperance in dealing with the object of your inquiry. Carefully measure your reactions by disengaging opinionated attitudes. Only in this way can you begin to make progress.

---

* Philosopher Lao Tzu best suggests the mood of moderation in the following excerpt from his small classic *Tao-te ching,* written in the sixth century B.C.:

> He who stands on tiptoe is not steady.
> He who strides forward does not go.
> He who shows himself is not luminous.
> He who justifies himself is not prominent.
> He who boasts of himself is not given credit.
> He who brags does not endure for long.

TOP LINE

Your inner development is not yet complete. The time calls for self-discipline. When difficulties arise, do not place the blame upon others. Once you begin to take responsibility for your own destiny you can bring order to your environment.

FIFTH LINE

Despite the mild balance that is reached in *MODERATION*, it may be necessary to take forceful action to accomplish your aims. This should not be done with a boastful display of power but with firm, decisive, and objective action. There will be improvement in whatever you undertake.

FOURTH LINE

Once the balance of true *MODERATION* is reached, it must be continually maintained. This does not mean simply maintaining the form of *MODERATION*, but continuing to cultivate equilibrium in your character and a sense of responsibility toward your society.

▶ THIRD LINE

With an unwavering commitment and hard work, you gain honor and fame. Do not allow such recognition to lead you astray or put you in a compromising position. Maintaining the perseverance that brought you prominence will win you continued support. You can then bring your work to completion.

SECOND LINE

By maintaining a careful inner *MODERATION*, your outward actions gain influence and weight. You will now be entrusted with responsibilities. A thoroughness in your actions brings good fortune.

BOTTOM LINE

If you can carry out your proposed endeavor quietly, competently, and thoroughly, without obvious announcements of your intentions, you can achieve even significant aims. With a modest and disciplined attitude, you do not create resistance or invite challenge.

16

YU

**ABOVE: CHEN
THUNDER**

**BELOW: K'UN
EARTH**

**UPPER: K'AN
WATER**

**LOWER: KEN
MOUNTAIN**

RULING LINES

*The ruling line in the fourth
position of social consciousness harmonizes the entire
hexagram.*

HARMONIZE
(ENTHUSIASM)

All events in nature follow the path of least resistance and harmonious natural order. Rivers cut through the most yielding areas in their downward rush to the oceans. The tides rhythmically undulate to the pull of the moon, while the moon orbits on the tether of the earth's gravity. The earth is held in check on its axis by the sun, and there follow the seasons in fixed regularity. All things in life *HARMONIZE* with these laws and patterns, including the myriad affairs of man.

Within society there are fixed traditions, popular opinions, and irresistible sympathies that instinctively spring from the nature of mankind. When you wish to lead, influence, govern, or arouse others, you must first align your values to those held by society. In this way you gain the attention, enthusiasm, and co-operation of others. Prohibitions that run contrary to the sentiment and life-style of people create resentment. Unpopular wars cannot be waged without shattering the public spirit and causing disharmony.

During this time you should seek to analyze the essential nature of the moment. If you can grasp the direction of the tendencies around you, you can parallel them and accomplish great deeds. New ideas, inventions, and innovations can now be successfully developed and promoted. Penetrate the popular sentiment of society, anticipate what will be needed and supported, and choose able helpers who will be enthusiastically attracted to your compelling inspiration.

The Chinese compared this time to the composition of music. The persuasive and mathematical purity of harmony in music inspires the hearts of the listeners in a mass experience. The forceful mystery of this tonal relationship can be demonstrated as an invisible language of our perceptions of reality. The profound experiences of art, education, history, healing, religion, and patriotism are expressed in music. People are inspired, in times of harmonizing, to feelings of universal perfection and truth. So powerful are these moments of perfect harmony that Confucius was prompted to say: "He who could wholly comprehend this sacrifice could rule the world as though it were spinning on his hand."

This hexagram suggests that you are now able to *HARMONIZE* socially and communicate fully your ideas and interests. Your general resonance with the mood of the time should make you particularly charismatic in your personal relationships.

You can now readily put yourself in touch with your true nature in order to further the development of your character. Pay attention to your bodily rhythms, observe your inherent character traits, and listen to your inner voice. Moreover, this state of mind can enhance your health and well-being. You can instill in your body an enthusiasm for life by harmonizing your spirit with the cosmic order.

The trigram, CHEN, movement, is influencing from above K'UN, receptivity, and inciting it to activity. Without change, your need to HARMONIZE is vital. Obey your inner voice if you wish to behave correctly in the current situation. If there is a decision to be made, surrender to the impulses of your true nature. Choose the path of least resistance. Move with the rhythm of the moment. In this way you will be relieved of tensions and open to inspired accord with the cosmos.

TOP LINE

The person in this position is lost in the memory of a compelling and harmonious experience. The time is past, and what is left is empty egotism. Fortunately, reform is possible. There is an opportunity to move on to a situation of new growth.

FIFTH LINE

Total harmony is obstructed and impossible. Yet the very awareness of this will keep you from sinking into chaos and eventual defeat.

▶ FOURTH LINE

Harmonious times are approaching. It is safe to exhibit your confidence in the future. Your attitude will attract others to you, who will co-operate in your endeavors. In this way you can accomplish great deeds.

THIRD LINE

You have waited complacently for a cue from someone else to motivate you. Whatever the reasons for your hesitation, whether it is idle pleasure in the present or simply inertia, you are losing your independence and self-reliance. You can still save yourself. Move.

SECOND LINE

To be able to recognize the early signs of a change in fortune is a tremendous gift. While others may be swept away by compelling rhythms and fads, you adhere firmly to the underlying principles of your nature and react appropriately to the demands of the time. Such is the behavior of leaders.

BOTTOM LINE

Although you may have a harmonious connection with someone in a high position, it does not necessarily indicate that you are on top of the situation. Furthermore, if you boast of your advantage, you will surely invite disaster.

17

SUI

ABOVE: TUI
LAKE

BELOW: CHEN
THUNDER

UPPER: SUN
WIND

LOWER: KEN
MOUNTAIN

RULING LINES

Both firm rulers place themselves beneath yielding positions. The ruler in the first position of beginning inspirations takes a subordinate place, as does the fifth line of authority.

ADAPTING
(FOLLOWING)

When autumn approaches, all of life that continues to survive begins an adaptation to the season. The pelts of animals begin to thicken in anticipation of the winter, while the seeds of plants scatter themselves in autumn winds to await the spring. The bark of the tree increases to protect itself from the cold, while insects may burrow deep inside to hibernate. By *ADAPTING* to the forces, life is protected as it rests and restores itself for new activity.

ADAPTING is knowing when to act and when to rest, when to speak and when to be silent. The nature of this hexagram is compared to the time of autumn when activity ebbs and rest begins. This is not a restraint, for there is no stress involved. It is instead a peaceful, accepting frame of mind willing to adjust to the existing forces. You should now concern yourself with doing the best you possibly can under the circumstances. Leave the control of the situation to others. Even if you feel you possess the strength to alter events, it is in your best interests to remain low. True power lies in serving others, and with such behavior comes progress and success.

In worldly matters, only leaders who adapt their vision to the sentiments of society will be followed. If their ideals are too far from the popular mainstream of reality, if they are not *ADAPTING* their product or service in the interests of the times, then following them can lead to danger. However, if their goals are harmonious with the times, you may commit yourself to their leadership. When you follow another, you may relax and restore yourself.

Try to be flexible in your social and personal relationships and, if necessary, subordinate yourself. It is correct to adapt to the situation presented now, for this is the only way that there will be favorable progress. Do not waste your energies struggling against the predominant forces. Instead, make your relationships as rewarding as possible by *ADAPTING* yourself to the current mood.

Rid yourself of old prejudices and opinions that may be controlling your behavior and holding you back. If your goals and principles are not consonant with those of your society, then you must make an adjustment in yourself. Your progress now depends upon the reality of your milieu. You may live by your own rules in your own home, but once outside, you must adapt. By *ADAPTING* to the realities around you at this time, you will find peace of mind and success.

By organically adapting itself, CHEN, *new growth, in the lower trigram finds satisfaction,* TUI, *as it enters the upper realm.* When *ADAPTING* occurs in a static form, it implies, without question, that no growth or progress can take place until the demands of the time are met. No situation can become favorable now, until you are a part of it. The nature of the time suggests that you cannot rule a situation until you first serve it. Do not struggle. Relax and adapt.

TOP LINE

You are called upon, by virtue of your wisdom and expertise, to lead another. You will unquestionably become involved, but you will be rewarded for your unselfish commitment.

▶ FIFTH LINE

If you sincerely insist upon the very best, the chances are that you will get it. Set your sights high. Good fortune.

FOURTH LINE

Those whom you appear to influence actually have ulterior motives in their allegiance to you. Look beyond the current flattering situation into your original principled aim. Strive to act independently.

THIRD LINE

You will find yourself parting ways with former inferior elements in your life as you make contact with worthwhile persons or ideals. By firmly following the superior path you will find what you are looking for, while your strength of character will greatly benefit.

SECOND LINE

Examine your goals and the standards you have set for yourself. If they are unworthy, inferior, weak, or nonexistent, you will remain low, and you will lose contact with productive, competent, worthwhile influences. You are forced to make a choice.

▶ BOTTOM LINE

A change is occurring, whether in your own objectives or in the situation around you. In order to accomplish something you should now communicate with persons of all persuasions and opinions. Yet remain internally principled and discerning.

18

KU

**ABOVE: KEN
MOUNTAIN**

**BELOW: SUN
WIND**

**UPPER: CHEN
THUNDER**

**LOWER: TUI
LAKE**

RULING LINES

*The fifth line in the position
of authority is yielding and
receptive and therefore capable of changing and or-
dering the entire hexagram.*

REPAIR
(DECAY)

The object of your inquiry is in a state of disrepair. This may be an inherited difficulty or it may have come about because you have been unaware of a need to constantly monitor, analyze, and attend to the details of the situation. You cannot ignore, or discount as unimportant, even the smallest detail of any situation over which you wish to maintain control. All things have built-in weak points, places that decay and eventually collapse. This is especially visible in human affairs.

Stop now and think about it. Your problems may seem to be overwhelming; things may appear to be out of hand. Yet the hexagram *REPAIR* bodes great success. Through work you have the opportunity to totally eliminate the past indifference that has created the present uncomfortable situation. Work hard. You can see the problems clearly. The timing is excellent for making amends. Do not be afraid to take assertive action. Outside forces do not influence the situation. Your own past attitude has allowed the damage to occur, making you uniquely equipped to *REPAIR* it.

Before taking action, it is important to consider the winding path that has led to this state of decay. Only through intelligent deliberation can you be certain that the action you take is correct. Think it over carefully. The original Chinese text recommends three days of consideration before making a move, but you will know when to act by the nature of what you propose to do. The correct actions now are constructive rather than combative and lay the foundation for continued growth toward the good. This is not a time for radical or reactionary reforms. Look, instead, for an avenue of constructive action, an area of positive growth. Be energetic once you've found your path of action. Don't be lulled into inertia by the magnitude of the task. The situation will develop new energy and inspiration once the problems are removed. Also remember that you must keep things in line once the change has been made. Don't slip back into an attitude of complacency. Your problems could easily recur.

This hexagram in its static form points to the necessity of a change in attitude about your environment as a whole. *Settled above, the mountainous weight of the trigram KEN, stillness, holds immovable SUN, the trigram of gentle effects.* Too many elements in your life have reached a state of neglect, disrepair, and inertia. You cannot hope to guide your destiny with any effectiveness when you do not have authority and control over everyday situations. Hope lies in an unrelentingly energetic and conscientious attitude.

TOP LINE

It is possible for you to transcend the entire situation. You do not have to deal with the mundane details of specific social problems. Instead, you may concern yourself with universal goals and personal or spiritual development. Caution: Viewing the world with a cynical or condescending eye, however, will distort your growth, so watch your attitudes carefully.

▶ FIFTH LINE

You are in a position to assume the responsibility for a long-needed reform. Do it. Those around you will be supportive of your efforts and you will be honored with praise and recognition.

FOURTH LINE

The situation has been less than harmonious for quite some time, yet this condition of discord has been tolerated. Under these circumstances things will continue to degenerate.

THIRD LINE

You are anxious to rectify the mistakes of the past and move vigorously into the future. Your actions may be hasty and you will be judged inconsiderate by others, but in the end you will not suffer for it.

SECOND LINE

You have become aware of past mistakes that must be rectified. Here you must proceed with great sensitivity, since the changes in your life could hurt those dear to you.

BOTTOM LINE

In order to avoid decay, it is necessary to change a traditional and rigid structure that is affecting your life. You may feel that this is too radical an undertaking. It is true that this kind of change is fraught with danger, but if you are cautious while making the reform you will meet with success and renewed growth.

19

LIN

**ABOVE: K'UN
EARTH**

**BELOW: TUI
LAKE**

**UPPER: K'UN
EARTH**

**LOWER: CHEN
THUNDER**

RULING LINES

The two firm lines at the bottom of the hexagram, in the positions of inspiration and self-interest, create the arousing atmosphere of PROMOTION. They rule jointly and aggressively.

PROMOTION
(APPROACH)

The time is one of immediate *PROMOTION*. The Chinese correlated this hexagram to the end of winter and the very beginning of spring. Like the sprout of a new plant shooting forth its first burst of creative activity, you can now make your first positive advancements toward the attainment of your goal.

If your concerns are directed toward matters of politics or power, this will be a most rewarding moment. A *PROMOTION* of your abilities or talents will now put you in the spotlight of events. At the same time, you will find yourself in a position of authority. You will be able to skillfully influence and support others. It would be wise to address yourself to the concerns of those around you, thus consolidating your position in society. This tremendously positive time will not last forever, so you must use it to its best advantage. The original text of the hexagram states: "When the eighth month comes there will be misfortune." This refers to the decline of autumn, which lies unavoidably ahead. Therefore you should make the most of this spring of power and optimism to prepare yourself for the natural cycle of decline.

There is a *PROMOTION* on the horizon in the affairs of business. If you have been waiting for an opportune moment to put forth a new idea or to maneuver yourself into a better position, the time has come. Those in authority have never been more receptive toward you. Great progress is a real possibility, and financial affairs are in your control as well. Use these advantages to make gains now and prepare for the future.

In your social world you have "arrived." Your charisma is powerful and you are able to influence and teach others to improve their own outlooks. This *PROMOTION* in social prominence should be used to enhance and invigorate your entire environment, thus preparing a secure foundation for any cultural regressions.

Relationships have the potential to blossom and you may find yourself in the role of the assertive partner. Your input can create the atmosphere for the strengthening of personal bonds. The time is most inspiring in matters of the heart because things are at their very beginning of development. Be tolerant and caring and you can build a structure that will weather those stormier emotional encounters that are a part of any relationship.

There is now a dynamic emphasis on inner growth. You will gain great clarity about your identity and your place in the larger scheme of things. Physical and spiritual strength will be enhanced as you sense a *PROMOTION* into new worlds of self-realization. Try to develop a permanent perspective of the confidence you are now experiencing to guide you through upcoming confusion or depression.

K'UN, *in the upper trigram of cosmic ideals, is receptive to* TUI, *joy and satisfaction, in the lower trigram of human affairs. PROMOTION without change suggests an eternal spring in regard to the object of your inquiry. This is indeed auspicious, as it appears that you are in an excellent position to carry out your plans successfully; or perhaps you can help others in the attainment of their own pursuits.*

TOP LINE

The person in this position will allow others to benefit from the wealth of his experience. Such generosity will bring unaccountable progress to all concerned. This is a true moment of greatness.

FIFTH LINE

Your position is one of sovereignty. Here you would be wise to allow others to execute your plan for you. If you can choose competent helpers and restrain yourself from interfering in their work, you will achieve the ideal of true authority.

FOURTH LINE

Your *PROMOTION* is well executed. Regardless of any difficulties you may encounter in assuming your new position, your behavior is so appropriate that you can continue successfully on your way.

THIRD LINE

An easy *PROMOTION* is possible now. This might lead to a careless attitude on your part. There is danger in such overconfidence. If you are quick to recognize the need for continuous caution, however, you can avoid mistakes that would otherwise harm you.

▶ SECOND LINE

What you propose to do wins sympathy and support from higher forces. So correct are your ideals that you can overcome even inherent difficulties. The future is bright indeed.

▶ BOTTOM LINE

Begin your endeavors in the company of those who share your enthusiasm. This will give you the kind of strong support necessary to achieve your aims. At the same time you should be certain that you are pursuing worthwhile goals. Continuing in your principles brings good fortune.

20

KUAN

**ABOVE: SUN
WIND**

**BELOW: K'UN
EARTH**

**UPPER: KEN
MOUNTAIN**

**LOWER: K'UN
EARTH**

RULING LINES

The hexagram resembles a mountain or temple. The correct ruler in the fifth position of authority holds together with the perspective of the ruler in the top position of wisdom. Authority with wisdom brings order to the hexagram.

CONTEMPLATING

The seasons of the year flow into one another with fixed regularity, deviating only within themselves but never in relation to one another. This regular pattern is evident in all phenomena from the movements of the solar system to the migration habits of the animals. All matter in the cosmos is subject to the same cyclic laws, the fates of civilizations and individuals being no exception. Therefore, by *CONTEMPLATING* the cosmic laws and their effects on both your life and the lives of others, you can gain an insight into the unfolding patterns of events. This perspective is extremely powerful, and the gifted individual can use it to master himself and his environment.

Just as the life of the individual is composed of seasons, the spring of inspiration, the summer of work, the autumn of completion and the winter of rest and contemplation, so too worldly events have their seasons. When attempting to determine the meaning and tendency of a situation at this time, approach it with the predictable plan of the seasons in mind. By *CONTEMPLATING* the present situation and taking note of what immediately preceded it, you should be able to determine what will follow.

The inherent ability to predict such tendencies is difficult to accept because one rarely sees what one desires. Yet the individual who can courageously and objectively contemplate in this way masters his world. He then becomes a part of the cosmic law, reacting instinctively and appropriately. Those around him are swept along by the force of his presence. Such a person is a true leader, for he leads not with force, but with divine inspiration.

Take this time of *CONTEMPLATING* to move freely through society. Experience new ideas fully, then offer your advice. Others will now listen eagerly to what you have to say. In matters of business, your ideas will have true impact. Use this opportunity to explore, contemplate, and modify any practices or policies that seem unsuitable. Your example, through honest contemplation, will create trust among your associates.

Your personal relationships will develop smoothly because you can grasp what is needed and respond properly. Through unity and co-operation you can expand these relationships into new areas of personal and social importance.

Keep in mind that at this time you are being contemplated by others as well. When you are in touch with the forces and laws of the cosmos, your position will become as prominent and obvious as your influence. The higher you rise in an attempt to see and contemplate, the more visible you become.

The upper trigram, SUN, *gentle effects, is successfully influencing* K'UN, *receptivity.* Without changing lines, the hexagram *CONTEMPLATING* indicates that there is work to be done in regard to the object of your inquiry. Seriously contemplate the situation and grasp its true meaning and direction of development. Once you understand it, influence and change it wherever necessary. Fear not. If you've aligned yourself realistically to the situation, you will be trusted.

▶ TOP LINE

You are somewhat beyond the situation and able to contemplate your life without egotistical involvement. You will discover, here, that freedom from error and blame are the highest good. Egoless contemplation is the key.

▶ FIFTH LINE

You will gain an understanding of what the future holds for you by *CONTEMPLATING* the effect of your life upon others. If your influence and example are good, then you are without blame. This, you will find, is its own reward.

FOURTH LINE

You can now progress by *CONTEMPLATING* society and determining the best cause, leader, or organization you can join or support. This social awareness and its enactment will further your growth, for you can transcend your position as one of the masses and exert significant influence.

THIRD LINE

In order to make the correct decisions in your life, you must gain objective self-knowledge. This is not accomplished by exploring your own dreams, attitudes, and opinions. These are useless in self-examination. Instead, contemplate your effect upon the world around you. There you will find yourself.

SECOND LINE

If you have goals more ambitious than maintaining your own private world, if your dreams extend into the affairs of society, then you must develop a broader viewpoint. If you relate everything that comes your way in terms of your own life and attitudes, you cannot develop.

BOTTOM LINE

Are you just looking at the surface of the situation and its most superficial effect upon you? This is an inferior, unenlightened form of contemplation. The superior mind will attempt to see the situation as part of a larger whole. This way you can know its actual meaning in your life.

21

SHIH HO

REFORM
(BITING THROUGH)

ABOVE: LI
FIRE

BELOW: CHEN
THUNDER

UPPER: K'AN
WATER

LOWER: KEN
MOUNTAIN

RULING LINES

Seen similarly to hexagram No. 27, as an open mouth, the fourth line is a blockage that must be removed. Also, it prevents the two nuclear trigrams from being receptive. The yielding ruler must be prodded into reforming the situation.

The time calls for energetic *REFORM*. Either an inferior person who is working against you or a situation that has developed at cross purposes to your life is interfering with the attainment of your aims. These obstacles must be sought out, reformed, and thereby eliminated. Success will come through the enforcement of laws and the administering of justice. There is neither possibility of compromise nor hope that the problem will miraculously vanish. It cannot be rationalized or ignored, and you cannot maneuver around it. It is a tangible, real, and self-generating interference in your life, and must be severely reformed before it causes any permanent damage to you.

In dealing with social and political affairs, a strict adherence to established justice is necessary. A society without principles or clarity about its laws is a group of people who are going nowhere. If you are a leader, then take the initiative to administer just, reasonable, and swift penalties to restore order; if you are a member, now is the time to support superior persons who can bring about social *REFORM*.

Personal relationships without defined guidelines, reasonable expectations, reciprocal considerations, and clear plans for the future are now in danger of dissolving in the chaos being generated by the current situation. Misunderstandings and confusions will become more common unless firm, clear headed action is taken to dispense with whatever you perceive to be an obstacle to union. There are times to avoid confrontations, to sublimate deep feelings, or to retreat and await a more opportune moment for action. This is not one of those times. Energetic *REFORM* will bring favorable results.

There could not be a more appropriate time to examine your character and determine the extent to which any delusions, rationalizations, or habits have usurped control of your judgment. Equivocal or vague principles, as a rule, will make of your life an undirected, uninspired, meaningless act. Know what you want, know what makes you feel good about your Self, know what brings you into harmony with others. These are your guidelines and principles. Other factors that assume control of your behavior or your health or that create inner discord are the obstacles that must be overcome. Be firm, unemotional, gentle, and clear in annihilating them and thereby *re-forming* your Self and your environment.

There is an inner storm that has been raging for some time around the object of your inquiry. *The lower trigram, CHEN, movement, is struggling upward, sparking brilliance in the upper trigram, LI. This dramatic coming together of the two strong elemental forces creates a tremendous cacophony and, eventually, release, just as thunder and lightning bring the release of static tensions before a storm.* Without changing lines, a radical *REFORM* is necessary in your life. It will cause spectacular reaction but will release the tensions that hold you back from your aims.

TOP LINE

A person who cannot recognize his own wrongdoings will drift farther and farther from the path. A person who is no longer on the path cannot understand the warnings of others. The original text states: "There will be evil."

▶FIFTH LINE

Even though there are few alternatives, a decision is difficult to make. Once you choose the course you will take, do not waver from your decision. Remain aware of the dangers and in this way you will surmount them.

FOURTH LINE

The task facing you is indeed difficult. That which you must overcome is in a powerful position. Be firm and persevering once you begin. Good results come only by being alert and exercising continuous effort.

THIRD LINE

You lack sufficient power and authority to bring about *REFORM*. Your attempts meet with indifference, and you may feel humiliated at your ineffective actions. Yet *REFORM* is necessary, and therefore your endeavors are justified.

SECOND LINE

Punishment and retribution come swiftly and thoroughly to the person who continues in wrong behavior. Even though it may seem overly severe, it will effectively bring about *REFORM*. Finally, there is no mistake in this.

BOTTOM LINE

Since this is only your first departure from the right path, only a mild punishment is forthcoming. This should serve the purpose of early *REFORM*.

22

PI

**ABOVE: KEN
MOUNTAIN**

**BELOW: LI
FIRE**

**UPPER: CHEN
THUNDER**

**LOWER: K'AN
WATER**

RULING LINES

*The yielding ruler in the
lower trigram of human affairs brings adornment and
GRACE to the surrounding
lines. The distant ruler in
the upper trigram of cosmic
ideals brings idealism and
the example of firmness to
the fourth and fifth lines.*

GRACE

There exists now a perfect moment of balanced, aesthetic form. The multiplicity of your current experiences can be glimpsed as a still and shimmering tableau. This all-pervasive elegance brings pleasure to the heart, clarity to the mind, and tranquillity to the soul. You are in a state of *GRACE*. Contemplating your environment with the extraordinary point of view offered at this exceptional time can give you a vision of the possible perfection in the world. Yet ambitious attempts to achieve such perfection would be a mistake, for this is idealism at its worst. Use this ephemeral moment of *GRACE* to contemplate and refine only your immediate surroundings. Do not make any major decisions now.

Your social world will unfold with luxurious ceremony and your awareness of your position will be enhanced by traditional social events. Keep in mind that now the emphasis is on form rather than content. Do not mistake one for the other. The perfect balance of *GRACE* and the fabulous insights it affords you will eventually pass. Such insights are only useful in adorning the present moment. They should not be used to determine and shape your future. There are inherent perils and pitfalls in the ideals of beauty and *GRACE*.

In worldly matters, continue in your long-standing principles and priorities. This state of *GRACE* can bring a new sophistication to the affairs of business or power, and the time may be used to enhance your position. Nevertheless, if there are significant or far-reaching decisions to be made, this is not the time to make them. Use this state of *GRACE* only to advance areas such as public relations and public image.

The heights of idealism are developing in your personal relationships. Your appreciation of the aesthetics in love can color your perceptions of all areas in your life. There is nothing wrong in this. Understand, however, that you are now perceiving the most idealistic aspects of love, where day-to-day concerns would bring certain disillusionment. Although a little emotional *GRACE* is a good thing in any relationship, it is neither the basis for marriage nor divorce.

GRACE is an enriching time in inner development and self-expression. Those involved in creative or artistic endeavors will find their work very satisfying. It is an inspiring time as ideas flow and the world seems to stand still. What is produced now appears to be divinely inspired. This moment of *GRACE* should be relished for the pleasure and good fortune it brings, but it should not become the pivotal experience for radical change. Instead, contemplate the perfection of the moment and lose your Self in the rare tranquillity of *GRACE*.

Stillness, KEN, *in the upper trigram of cosmic ideals brings illumination and clarity,* LI, *to the lower trigram of human affairs. GRACE* in an unmoving form suggests that the moment is isolated in time. While you can see the true perfection that might be in the situation of your inquiry, it is not necessarily consonant with reality. You are dealing with idealisms. There is no redemption in your illusions, however fervently you feel them. The perfection in the heavens has put stars in your eyes.

▶ TOP LINE

You can rely now upon the sincerity of your true nature to supply your external radiance. Pretensions, form, and adornments are no longer necessary to achieve your aims. Simplicity is the path you must take. In this way you will make no mistakes.

FIFTH LINE

You may wish to strenghten your connection with someone you admire, but you feel that what you have to offer is not grand enough to merit attention. However, your internal desires and sincere feelings of friendliness are all that truly matter. Your worth will be recognized and you will meet with good fortune.

FOURTH LINE

You have a choice of two paths. One is the path of adornment and external brilliance; the other is the path of simplicity and inner worth. Your considerations suggest a deeper connection with your true Self. The path of simplicity will lead to more meaningful relationships with others and greater self-knowledge.

THIRD LINE

You are in a moment of perfect *GRACE*, living a charmed existence. Do not allow such good fortune to make you indolent, for this would bring unhappiness. Continue to persevere in your endeavors and principles.

▶ SECOND LINE

GRACE for its own sake is worthless to you now. It is merely an adornment. If you pay more attention to the vessel than to what it contains, you will entirely miss the meaning of this moment.

BOTTOM LINE

Move forward under your own power and avoid false appearances, dubious shortcuts, or ostentatious behavior. It is most important now that you rely upon your own worth.

23

PO

**ABOVE: KEN
MOUNTAIN**

**BELOW: K'UN
EARTH**

**UPPER: K'UN
EARTH**

**LOWER: K'UN
EARTH**

RULING LINES

▶

The structure of the hexagram shows yielding lines about to undermine the final firm line. The ruler at the top position of wisdom is benevolent toward the lines below and maintains its strength.

DETERIORATION
(SPLITTING APART)

There is an impressive display of *DETERIORATION* in nearly every aspect of the current affair. These lesser elements, and those who represent them, have gained complete control over the situation. *DETERIORATION* will continue to spread until it falls out of fashion, and there is nothing a person of integrity can do but wait. Eventually there will come a change for the better.

In political affairs and matters of power the time may be thought of as a rapid *DETERIORATION* or overthrow. There exists now an abundance of incompetent persons in positions of authority to help bring this about. As shown in the extraordinarily long period of recorded history in ancient China, where the *I Ching* was often used as a political manual, such declines were expected and accepted. The original text of the hexagram states: "The superior man respectfully appreciates the cycles of increase and decrease, of greatness and decadence, as revealed by the heavenly bodies." The text continues to warn against forging ahead at this time. Your best course is to wait out the difficult times and protect yourself by generously providing for those close to you.

The time should be contemplated with great care in all financial and business matters. If possible, do nothing to progress your own interests. You will simply be advancing into adversity and possibly disaster. The situation is in the hands of persons lacking in vision. Wait until things change and concern yourself, meanwhile, with insuring your own position. Reach out benevolently and consolidate your relationships with those below you. This will provide for you a secure foundation while you wait.

This is a difficult time socially, for fulfilling communications with others are in a state of *DETERIORATION* as well. In social interactions, a low profile will help you avoid misunderstandings. If you are an artist or involved in influencing your milieu, you could not pick a more unfortunate time to seek an audience. If you have the opportunity to overlook a social event, do so.

If there is a breach in your personal relationships, it cannot be easily bridged now. Remain calm and quiet for the present, and if you can, be generous and supportive of those dear to you. Then, when things improve, as they naturally will, you will find that you have preserved and strengthened your relationships.

At this time your health and inner development may be in a less than ideal state due to inferior elements in your environment. Yet external ploys will not put an end to the natural cycle of *DETERIORATION*. Time will. Nurture your mind and body reasonably and sensibly now. Look for wisdom in your acceptance of the times.

The lower trigram, K'UN, *submission, yields to the presence of* KEN, *immovability, above.* When *DETERIORATION* is received without changing lines it implies a situation for which there is little hope. It is not in your control, and therefore your interests are not considered. Reaffirm and support your position by being benevolent toward others. If there is a way out, it lies in a submissive attitude.

▶ TOP LINE

The forces of *DETERIORATION* have ended. The power will return to persons of worthwhile vision, who will again win the support of others. Inferior persons are destroyed by their own evil, for without power, negativity is self-consuming.

FIFTH LINE

An inferior situation is beginning to change for the better. Through co-operation, opposing forces can come together for mutual benefit. There is now a possibility for success in your endeavors.

FOURTH LINE

You are exposed to danger. Calamity is imminent and you are unable to hold it back. Without warning, you are on the threshold of defeat.

THIRD LINE

Circumstances have led you into a situation in which you must work with inferior persons or ideals. If you can, nevertheless, maintain a strong tie with a superior element, you will avoid *DETERIORATION* and free yourself of regretful errors.

SECOND LINE

The time requires the utmost caution. You are without allies in a compromising situation. Adapt as best you can to the circumstances. Do not take a self-righteous position or you could be badly hurt.

BOTTOM LINE

Your position is being undermined. Persons of inferior persuasions have entered the situation from below and are creating an environment for *DETERIORATION*. The time bodes evil for persons of integrity. All you can do is patiently wait.

24

FU

**ABOVE: K'UN
EARTH**

**BELOW: CHEN
THUNDER**

**UPPER: K'UN
EARTH**

**LOWER: K'UN
EARTH**

RULING LINES

▶

The ruling line is in the bottom position of inclination, the emphasis thus RETURNING to the beginning of the trigram of human affairs.

RETURNING

You are *RETURNING* to the beginning of yet another cycle in your life, after what may have seemed a long period of stagnation or frustration. Progress had been halted at every turn, and movement appeared impossible. Now the paths leading to renewed growth are revealing themselves. Although you may be quite anxious to proceed with your plans, you must keep in mind that things are just at their beginnings. Don't push. The improving situation will continue to develop at its own pace. This promising turn for the better is certain, and as natural as the change from a still, cold winter to the early anticipation of spring. And, like the seasons, the cycles in life cannot be hastened. Conserve your energies instead. You'll need them to cope with the inevitable complexities that arise with new phases. The *RETURNING* situation will establish itself of its own accord. Contemplate and adjust your relationship to this new phase in order to afford yourself a comfortable position within it.

This is a time when groups of like-minded individuals can come together and work toward a common goal. Success is indicated here because the progress of these individuals is unhampered, both in the external world and in their innermost motivations.

You may be experiencing a dormant period in your social life, or perhaps an illness that has held you back. This situation suggests a return to better times, but cautions as well against overly vigorous movement. Just because you feel better now, do not immediately throw yourself into an energetic undertaking or attempt to be the center of the social event of the season. Remember, you must strengthen the beginning with rest.

The time of *RETURNING* can also indicate a new beginning through a fresh approach to important relationships. If such is the case, treat this time very carefully. You must now be aware of what to expect from relationships that do not start out on the proper footing. Above all, this footing must be relevant to your nature. If you are still uncertain about this, this current phase is an ideal opportunity for self-knowledge. At the time of *RETURNING* to new beginnings is the implied *end* of an old cycle. Study the phase you are now exiting. It is a cycle. It had a beginning and you are experiencing its end. The reasons for certain things that may have been unacceptable or confusing to you are now apparent. The contemplation of the return of these cycles can lead to profound inner knowledge. The Chinese refer to this hexagram as the apparent pattern of the intelligence of Heaven and Earth.

Unchanging, this situation can mean the *RETURNING* to the beginning of one of your familiar old cycles or patterns. *The trigram* CHEN, *movement, is arousing from below* K'UN, *receptivity, into a repeated cycle of activity.* Throughout your life you will recognize occurrences that are not simply random, but a part of your own particular pattern. You may perceive this all too familiar pattern as neurotic or, perhaps, as the security of being your Self. Naturally, the better your attitude about certain fated conditions in your nature, the more pleasurable your life becomes.

TOP LINE

You've missed the time to make a change for the better at the beginning of this recent cycle. This is unfortunate because you were quite capable of recognizing the need for reform. Instead, you have stubbornly locked yourself into a nonconstructive attitude. You must now wait out the entire cycle before you have another chance to change.

FIFTH LINE

You are aware of the need for a new beginning and have the courage to make the change. By observing your faults with objectivity and resolution at this time you will gain the strength of character necessary to overcome them.

FOURTH LINE

Your current milieu is inferior. You have become aware of the possibility of a change for the better and wish to move in that direction. Be aware that your friends may not follow you. Your path could be a solitary one.

THIRD LINE

This position indicates the type of person who is constantly vacillating because of the imagined advantages of other paths. This kind of experimentation could be dangerous, but is mostly an annoyance to all concerned. It is indicated that the situation will improve nevertheless.

SECOND LINE

It is much easier to do the right thing when you are in good company. Following good examples will lead you to success.

▶ BOTTOM LINE

You may be considering an idea that is by nature contrary to your principles. Exercise self-discipline and hold to what you feel is right. In this way you cultivate your character and will surely attain great things.

25

WU WANG

**ABOVE: CH'IEN
HEAVEN**

**BELOW: CHEN
THUNDER**

**UPPER: SUN
WIND**

**LOWER: KEN
MOUNTAIN**

RULING LINES

▶

▶

*The firm line at the bottom
rules from the position of
instinct. The ruling line in
the fifth place of authority is
thus stimulated by innocent
urges.*

无
妄

INNOCENCE

The time demands an alignment with the flow of the cosmos. This adjustment must be made before further action is taken, otherwise you will begin to make mistakes. When actions that seem perfectly reasonable and cleverly planned are executed, they will end in difficulty and confusion. In order to harmonize your actions with the cosmos, it will be necessary to adopt an attitude of *INNOCENCE*. Examine your motives. They will be the cause of your problems. This is a time for acting without conscious purpose, without ulterior motive and with complete rectitude. Do not aspire to be rewarded for your actions, nor direct them cunningly toward personal advancement. Act innocently and react spontaneously.

Your instincts should be developed and modified in the direction of natural goodness. Your first inclinations should be to preserve your well-being, clear the way for your fellow man, and take note of worthwhile information. Without integrity and morality in your character you could not trust your instincts, for they might lead you into dangerous situations.

The path to your goal is now an indirect path. You must rely on your principles and inner virtue rather than clever strategies. This will not lead you away from success — on the contrary, *INNOCENCE* with spontaneity will bring creativity to many areas of your life. You will appear to your milieu inspired and brilliant. This will give you great influence. If you are a teacher, leader, or head of a family, use the insights and inspirations that will occur during a time of *INNOCENCE* to fulfill the needs of those who rely upon you. Do this without thought of compensation or hope of a possible gain in stature.

It is important to keep in mind that laws of the cosmos are divine and do not necessarily follow the desires of man. Therefore, when acting in *INNOCENCE*, you will also experience the unexpected, the exceptional, the unpredictable. Be prepared for a surprising turn of events. What occurs will stimulate new ideas, even if at first this seems unnerving or full of complications.

A state of *INNOCENCE* could be a refreshing interlude in your personal relationships. Spontaneity can bring great pleasure as well as reveal true feelings and motives, whereas intrigue at this time would only yield perplexity and possibly disaster. Again, *INNOCENCE* may lead to surprising new areas of unexplored mutual interest.

For those who are puzzled or at a standstill in regard to a particular issue, a spontaneous method of action could lead to a highly creative and original solution. Act without guile and do not attack the problem directly.

Spontaneous creativity in the upper trigram, CH'IEN, *is aroused and amplified by strong movement below in the trigram* CHEN. When there are no changing lines, the element of the unexpected is amplified. You may rest assured that whatever happens will not be at all what you expected. An accommodating attitude will see you through without error.

TOP LINE

Progress is impossible. Even innocent actions will create chaos. Do not attempt anything new, nor try to improve upon your surroundings. Do not do anything at all.

▶ FIFTH LINE

What may appear as an unfortunate turn of events has internal causes. External remedies will not solve the problem. What is occurring is an inner process. Let nature take its course. The solution will come of itself.

FOURTH LINE

Do not be influenced by the designs of those around you. It is very important, at this time, that you trust your inner vision. Obey your instincts.

THIRD LINE

Undeserved and unexpected misfortune may come your way. It will pass. An attitude of *INNOCENCE* does not preclude bad luck, as such shifts of fortune are unavoidable. However, an innocent posture should not be abandoned for it can reveal new ways of dealing with problems.

SECOND LINE

Do not dream about the results of your work or the attainment of your goal. Instead, take action for its own sake and devote your full attention to what you are now doing. Only in this way can you achieve your aim.

▶ BOTTOM LINE

Acting with integrity and spontaneity will bring you success. You may trust your instincts, because there is goodness in your heart. Good fortune is willed.

26

TA CH'U

**ABOVE: KEN
MOUNTAIN**

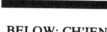

**BELOW: CH'IEN
HEAVEN**

**UPPER: CHEN
THUNDER**

**LOWER: TUI
LAKE**

RULING LINES

The ruler in the fifth position of authority yields to the strong ruler at the top. This top line has power and firmness in the position of wisdom. Together these lines have the qualities for potentially great achievements.

POTENTIAL ENERGY
(THE TAMING POWER OF THE GREAT)

Because you are in possession of a great deal of stored or *POTENTIAL ENERGY*, you may now undertake ambitious and far reaching endeavors. The timing of such efforts is of vast importance. The ability to control, direct, restrain, or store your powers will bring you very good fortune. Also, the continual re-evaluation of the correctness or worth of your plan is now a concern of major significance.

If you are considering issues that pertain to political matters, you should choose the path of public mindedness rather than personal advancement. Place your *POTENTIAL ENERGY* at the disposal of a worthy leader. You can work toward the fulfillment of a cause or social ideology with assured success. The time lends itself to the attainment of great achievements. When in doubt, give thought to the historical doctrines upon which current political systems are based.

You will find that the affairs of business lean toward the interests of public service. Any endeavors that provide goods and services that directly benefit others will meet with great success. You have at your disposal the accumulated knowledge or resources to launch a significant commercial enterprise. Be certain, however, that your objectives are worthwhile in the overall scheme of things. This is too great a time to waste on frivolous ventures.

Bear with even difficult social relationships and attempt to cultivate useful connections. This time of *POTENTIAL ENERGY* can lend astonishing dimensions to your circle of influence. You can skillfully organize others into a useful network of social exchange. Artists and those involved in creative communications will benefit greatly by expanding their worlds. The emphasis now should be on pragmatic and useful communications.

You possess a storehouse of potential psychological energy. There is no reason that it should not be used in a positive exchange. Personal relationships could blossom overnight. For greatest success, hold to traditional values. View all feelings in the light of what has come before and what is expected by tradition.

Pay particular attention to the continuing development of your character. The totality of what you have experienced has organized itself into an illuminated perspective of great clarity. This may be a real breakthrough in the maturing process. You have the *POTENTIAL ENERGY* for an enlightened insight that could change your life.

The great weight of still meditation, KEN, *in the upper trigram contains tremendous creative force,* CH'IEN, *below. POTENTIAL ENERGY in its static form is explosive. You will have to very carefully release the restraining pressures. Look for guidance in an experienced person who holds a position of authority or in historically sound organizations or methods. Act now.*

►TOP LINE

All obstacles give way. *POTENTIAL ENERGY* can be used to accomplish great deeds in the world. Align yourself with the *tao* and you will meet with unparalleled success.

►FIFTH LINE

By cutting off the roots of an uncontrolled great force, it can be restrained and redirected. This indirect approach is much better than direct combat or confrontation. Good fortune.

FOURTH LINE

That which has held you back has, in fact, aided in your growth. Instead of squandering your resources on premature advancements, you have built up a strong reserve of *POTENTIAL ENERGY*. Good fortune.

THIRD LINE

The path will begin to open for you, and your progress will be unhindered. Others may join forces with you. Nevertheless, you must constantly keep your personal goals in mind. Remain cautious.

SECOND LINE

There is no opportunity for advancement. You are held back by forces that are beyond your reach. Stay where you are and continue to build the resources of your *POTENTIAL ENERGY*. Be content with the present situation. There should be no conflict.

BOTTOM LINE

Compose yourself. You may feel that you are restrained from advancing. In fact, there are obstacles on the path ahead. It would be wise to halt.

27

I

**ABOVE: KEN
MOUNTAIN**

**BELOW: CHEN
THUNDER**

**UPPER: K'UN
EARTH**

**LOWER: K'UN
EARTH**

RULING LINES

*The lines form the shape of
an open mouth, thus the
idea of NOURISHING. The
fifth line of authority is receptive (yielding) to the top
line of wisdom; therefore
they rule and nourish the
hexagram wisely.*

NOURISHING

The idea of the hexagram *NOURISHING* originates from the interdependent structure of the food cycle on earth. All of life is sustained within a self-perpetuating system. An example of this system is the balanced exchange of oxygen, carbon dioxide, and nitrogen among plants, animals, and earth. At the same time, the quality and quantity of this *NOURISHING* exchange yields a particular quality and quantity of growth.

The correct *NOURISHING* of yourself and others is the focus of this time. When your endeavors involve the *NOURISHING* of others, it is important that they are worthy of such support. If you consistently nourish superior persons, who will in turn provide nourishment for others, you can achieve great effects. Through nurturing and support, social and political aims can meet with success.

In judging another person or situation, the model of *NOURISHING* is an excellent analytical device. Out of poor habits or erroneous thinking a man may nourish himself in an inferior way. This pattern may be detected by observing his outstanding character traits. If they are inferior traits, then he takes into himself inferior things and will have nothing to offer you. If his character traits are worthy of praise, that which he chooses to ingest is superior and he may have much that is worthwhile to give.

If there are difficulties in your relationship, take note of the quality of what you give to others. Do you offer inspiration or discouragement? Do you focus on what is wrong with particular situations or on what could be right? The correct *NOUR-ISHING* of those close to you is vital to your sense of well-being, for such supportive activity will ultimately come back to you in kind. This cycle of *NOURISHING* will have an indirect yet profound impact on your life.

Additionally, you should exercise unrelenting discipline over your thought patterns. Cultivate only productive opinions and attitudes in order to properly nourish your character. If you are engaged in activity at this time, keep your mind as calm and relaxed as possible. Avoid excited and opinionated outbursts; instead, express yourself with moderation. Pay special attention to what you allow to enter your sphere of awareness, and, at the same time, avoid excessive indulgences.

You are the product of everything you put into your body and mind. In its static form, *NOURISHING* is perfectly balanced. *The upper trigram, KEN, stillness, meditates upon the new growth quickened by the lower trigram, CHEN, arousing.* If you are satisfied with the state of your inquiry, then continue your input habits, for they are producing the current situation. If you are discontent you must seriously alter your appetites.

▶ TOP LINE

The person in this position has a highly developed awareness of what is required in order to properly educate, influence, and nourish others. Should he undertake this task, conscious of all the implications of his responsibilities, he will bring happiness to many.

▶ FIFTH LINE

Although you are aware of the need to nourish and affect others, you lack sufficient strength to do so unaided. You must take an indirect approach and depend upon a strong superior to accomplish the deed. Don't try it on your own.

FOURTH LINE

Any desire to energetically nourish others will meet with success. You are in a position to be supportive and influential, although you may need to enlist help. Look for clever people to aid you. There is no mistake in this.

THIRD LINE

You cannot be fully nourished because you are too busy looking for nourishment in the wrong places. In doing this, you turn away from others who might help you, and therefore you achieve nothing. This is eccentric and dangerous behavior.

SECOND LINE

Although you are able to properly nourish yourself in this situation, you rely upon inappropriate methods or persons to fulfill your needs. If this continues, it will rob you of your independence and create an unhealthy state of mind. Difficulties will follow.

BOTTOM LINE

You are so actively aware of the prosperity of others that you lose control of your own destiny. This is deplorable behavior and will result in misfortune.

28

TA KUO

ABOVE: TUI
LAKE

BELOW: SUN
WIND

UPPER: CH'IEN
HEAVEN

LOWER: CH'IEN
HEAVEN

RULING LINES

The hexagram is yielding and weak at the ends and firm and heavy in the center, creating a CRITICAL MASS. Unusual strength in the second position of self-interest and the fourth position of social consciousness generates ruling qualities.

CRITICAL MASS
(PREPONDERANCE OF THE GREAT)

In an atom, when *CRITICAL MASS* is reached, it is a time when several heavy particles are occupying the same space, thereby creating extraordinary events and catastrophic chain reactions. In much the same way, the current situation is becoming weighted with a great many considerations. There are numerous decisions pending, the air is full of ideas with all their ensuing multifarious possibilities, and the ponderous affairs of the people around you are pushing into the foreground. All of it is important, serious, and meaningful, and all of it is coming to a head right now.

Your environment is rapidly becoming the meeting ground for many of the major circumstances affecting you. These things will take up a great deal of your time, space and energy. More and more of your attention will be demanded by these very real imperatives. There is a lot going on, the situation is excessive and may reach *CRITICAL MASS* soon.

Look for an avenue of escape. Prepare to make decisions about your next move. Carefully evaluate all of the things affecting you. You will need your wits about you to successfully make this transition. Have a goal or destination in mind.

In social or business affairs make a rapid assessment of your situation. Concern yourself with the care and development of your assets. These are the things that you will carry away with you, and they should become the foundations of your character. Be ready to make a quick transition into an entirely new mode of life.

When experiencing *CRITICAL MASS* in personal relationships and inner development you must realize that this may be a time of crisis. Naturally, all that is coming to a head cannot be put off, but you should marshal your forces and penetrate the meaning of what is happening. If necessary, retreat into your innermost Self and attempt to comprehend your position. When several significant things come upon you at once, you must be prepared to take a stand and rely on the resilience of your character to see you through. If it should happen that you must face this alone and, in fact, renounce your entire milieu, you should do so confidently and courageously. Times like these bring to light the true fiber of the Self. A person who is prepared for momentous times will survive them unscathed and emerge even stronger.

Above all, when *CRITICAL MASS* is imminent, action must be taken. Whether this is a carefully considered escape or a resolute determination to dispense with what is to come, success surrounds those who remain strong and certain within.

In an unchanging form the time of *CRITICAL MASS* suggests that you may have to act alone and firmly during the onslaught of these weighted times. *The steady efforts of the lower trigram, SUN, hold firmly, while TUI, excess, predominates above.* There are times when too much of even a good thing is just *too much.*

TOP LINE

The goal is worth accomplishing, although the sacrifice to attain it may be confounding in its enormity. No blame is attached to such action, although you should realize the extraordinary reality of what is happening.

FIFTH LINE

In critical or significant times it is exhausting to cling to your ideals and ignore the realities of your environment. These realities are the superstructure that supports your life. If you ignore your foundations in your reach upward, you will become unstable and accomplish nothing at all.

▶ FOURTH LINE

You can now find within yourself the strength and vision to achieve a successful outcome in your endeavors. Do not rely upon people or things outside of your Self for guidance. Dependence now on external things leads to humiliation.

THIRD LINE

You are inclined to force your way forward when, in fact, there are obstacles that cannot be overcome in this way. Even worse, you cannot accept advice from others because it is not what you wish to hear. Misfortune will inevitably follow.

▶ SECOND LINE

Look to those who are modest in attitude, or are beginners themselves, to help you in your endeavors. This way you are in the company of persons who can understand and share the enthusiasm of your goals. Things will move smoothly and the situation will become revitalized.

BOTTOM LINE

When embarking on an important endeavor, it is necessary to pay particular attention to details at the beginning. The times are indeed extraordinary, and you must be particularly careful to proceed in the right way. Being overly cautious is not a mistake.

29

K'AN

**ABOVE: K'AN
WATER**

**BELOW: K'AN
WATER**

**UPPER: KEN
MOUNTAIN**

**LOWER: CHEN
THUNDER**

RULING LINES

The firm rulers in the centers of the two component trigrams are surrounded by yielding or weak lines. Although this is dangerous, they remain firm and auspicious.

DANGER

The situation is one of real *DANGER*, caused by and manifested in the affairs of man. This *DANGER* is not inspired by overwhelming tendencies within the cosmos, or by conflicts in your innermost attitudes. The real *DANGER* that confronts you is brought about by your immediate environment. It will take skill to overcome the difficulties, but managed properly, this time of challenge can bring out the very best in you. The Chinese text points out that if you can act with confidence and virtue whatever you do results in success.

Do not avoid confrontations in any difficult or threatening situations; you must now meet and overcome them through correct behavior. Maintain a continued resolve. Hold to your ethics and principles and do not for a moment consider compromising what you believe to be right. Acting with integrity and confidence is the key to surmounting the *DANGER*.

In business or political affairs, stick to approved policy. When making judgments regarding matters of leadership, neither bargain with your principles nor attempt to avoid the issue, for such actions would render meaningless all that has been achieved thus far. In social interactions, remain true to your nature. If possible, convince others of the soundness of your ideas by demonstrating the good effects of your actions. If they will not support you, you do not need them. Keep moving. Do not dally in the *DANGER*. In personal relationships, do not allow passions to lead you into peril. If the difficulties cannot be resolved without sacrificing your principles, the relationship may be irresolute.

The time of *DANGER* can be especially good for inner development. By holding to fixed and virtuous ethics, by maintaining your inner vision and ideals, all things will fall into a steady, tangible perspective. You will *know* your relationships to your environment, and in this way you can accomplish your aims. Although subjective, this perspective is now in accord with the problems facing you.

Additionally, by persevering in high-minded conduct, you become a living example to your family and your fellow man. Through the consistency of your actions you guide and inspire others in the handling of their own affairs. This in turn will create order and dispel *DANGER* within your milieu. Thus you are protected.

Frequent encounters with *DANGER* are a part of life. Beyond making you inwardly strong, familiarity with *DANGER*, like the near brush of death, can instill in you a profound awareness of the life force and the mysterious nature of the cosmos. Such heightened awareness can bring new meaning, determination, and richness into your life.

The component trigram is doubled. K'AN, *the dangerous and profound, is repeated above and below. In its static form,* DANGER *is repeated dramatically in regard to your inquiry. Your desires lead you into* DANGER *again and again. Repeatedly you manage an escape only to be confronted with another dangerous situation. Virtuous conduct, by strengthening your character, may help you transcend the entire affair.*

TOP LINE

None of your solutions or efforts have been appropriate. The way out of *DANGER* is blocked. There will come a long time of disorder. All you may do is wait.

▶ FIFTH LINE

Only struggle as much as necessary to extricate yourself from your problems. Overly ambitious persons who attempt more than they should may create further difficulties. It is indicated here that the *DANGER* will pass of its own accord.

FOURTH LINE

Take the simple and direct approach to solving your problems and overcoming difficulties. Strive for clarity of mind. Do not clutter your actions with useless pretense, since it will only confuse the situation.

THIRD LINE

You are surrounded by *DANGER* and you do not understand it. Any action will only make matters worse. Maintain your principles and wait for the solution to reveal itself.

▶ SECOND LINE

The *DANGER* is great and cannot be surmounted with one single action. Small, consistent efforts to stay afloat in a sea of difficulties are all that are possible at this time.

BOTTOM LINE

You have become accustomed to evil influences and no longer fight them. This could be the result of a weakness in your character. In any event, you've lost your way. The more action you take, the farther afield you'll stray. Begin again at another time.

30

LI

**ABOVE: LI
FIRE**

**BELOW: LI
FIRE**

**UPPER: TUI
LAKE**

**LOWER: SUN
WIND**

RULING LINES

*The rulers in the centers of
the repeated trigrams work
together in dependence. The
second position of self-interest brings correctness,
and the fifth position of authority brings receptivity
through its yielding nature.*

SYNERGY
(THE CLINGING)

When two elements approach each other in such a way that the scope of what they can achieve together far surpasses the total of what they could achieve separately, they are acting with *SYNERGY. SYNERGY,* in this case, takes the effectiveness of co-operation beyond normal expectations.

This hexagram suggests that you and the object of your inquiry are dependent upon each other. Working together, the interaction of your spheres of influence can achieve significant deeds. These synergetic interactions will provide ideas and in-spirations, generate surplus energy for continued growth, and refine com-munications and perceptions.

In worldly affairs, this is a time when a leader, dependent upon his principles and his sense of correctness, can bring enlightenment and order to those whom he leads. Here the *SYNERGY* between a leader and his integrity yields benefits to the people. The Chinese point out here: "Clarity of mind brought about by dependence on what is right can transform the world and perfect it."

In personal relationships you will find that the alignment of your desires can now achieve a great deal. This is a good time to examine your relationships and note whether you are working against one another or with *SYNERGY.* Co-operative efforts will not take energy away from individual pursuits. In fact, working relationships should now be especially supportive of individual achievements.

Keep in mind that as an individual your relationship with the cosmos is conditioned. By nature, the earth is a place of limitations — limitations of energy, of ideas, of resources, and even of the life force itself. The best way to achieve your aims within the limitations of your situation is to depend upon and synergize your energies with the forces of the cosmos. Learn to recognize the times, and act accordingly. When pressures mount, don't become explosive. Instead, work quietly and diligently to alleviate them. At times of high energy, don't throw yourself away in undisciplined euphoria. Work toward making the best use of the energy to enact new ideas and further your goals. When energies subside, use the time to rest and gather your strength instead of exhausting yourself with useless struggling. The development of *SYNERGY* within the Self will give you added dimensions of control over your future.

The hexagram SYNERGY is composed of the trigram, LI, dependence, doubled. Dependence below, furthering and co-operating with dependence above, will bring clarity to the situation. In an unchanging form, you must concentrate upon aligning the many elements in your life into synergetic accord in order to fully comprehend and control them. Goals, loved ones, career, and health: Do they all work together? Do they relate? Do they further one another? By achieving inner clarity, you bring enlightenment to the world.

TOP LINE

It is up to you to penetrate to the source of trouble in the situation and eradicate it. Act with moderation however, in dealing with others who may have been duped into wrong thinking. Once the major problem is out of the way, order will reign. (Note: This line may refer to a bad habit or character weakness.)

▶ FIFTH LINE

A true change of heart is occurring. Such dramatic change is sometimes accompanied by a deep grief. Yet with this grief comes good fortune because the change will bring better times for all concerned.

FOURTH LINE

Your display of overly enthusiastic energies and endeavors will exhaust you. Nothing will come of it all.

THIRD LINE

The best attitude to cultivate at this time in your life is a general acceptance of fate. To totally lose yourself in the happiness of the moment is as bad as to bemoan the passing of time. Such folly of the mind and the emotions leads to a loss of inner freedom. Misfortune.

▶ SECOND LINE

A reasonable and moderate attitude will bring you the best possible luck. Remember, indulge in no excess, no extremes of thought or action.

BOTTOM LINE

When you first begin on your new path, you are bombarded by impressions. Keep your goal in mind constantly and you can avoid confusion. Furthermore, do not forget your position as a beginner, somewhat outside the situation.

31

HSIEN

**ABOVE: TUI
LAKE**

**BELOW: KEN
MOUNTAIN**

**UPPER: CH'IEN
HEAVEN**

**LOWER: SUN
WIND**

RULING LINES

*The unusually strong ruler
in the fourth position of social concerns attracts and
influences the ruler in the
fifth position of authority.
They are paralleled and
united.*

ATTRACTION

The universe as we know it is held together and governed by the various laws of *ATTRACTION*. From the vast movements of the solar system in infinite space to the perfectly balanced center of the atom, these mutual attractions create all things. In life, these attractions manifest themselves in a complex network of desire, persever-ance, and fulfillment. Life begets life and evolves itself in an ordered and divine fashion. The *ATTRACTION* between mates, with an underlying interest toward so-cial unity and, perhaps, progeny, is the emphasis here. This magnetism is not a super-ficial desire. It is the beginning of the most basic social unit, the family, just as the atom, with the *ATTRACTION* of its positive and negative charges, is the basic mate-rial unit.

This is a serious and profound *ATTRACTION* that is shared by both you and the object of your interest, whether it is a person or a situation in which you are inte-grally involved in the outcome. In this situation you happen to be in the position of power. The initiative is yours. For the most successful results, you must subordinate yourself and free your mind of motive and prejudice. Allow the object of your inter-est to influence and change you. In this way, because of the advantage of your strength, *ATTRACTION* is reciprocal and the relationship or involvement is consum-mated.

This describes the way great leaders can influence society. An attitude of servitude demonstrated by the leader toward the people encourages them to ap-proach him for advice and guidance. In this way the leader can direct others into areas of greater development and order.* In social matters, your willingness to be influenced, even though you may be altogether self-sufficient, attracts others to you and creates an atmosphere for the exchange of ideas. Pertaining to personal relationships, it is unequivocally stated in the original text: "To take a spouse brings good fortune."

If you are attempting at this time to make a decision or judgment concerning another person, pay particular attention to what he attracts. In this way you can penetrate his nature and fate. By examining his energies, ideas and associations, you can begin to see what the nature of your involvement will be. Then you may deter-mine if such an *ATTRACTION* will benefit you. The same holds true in the judg-ment of any situation. By penetrating that which the situation attracts — people, problems, and possibilities — you can see the way it will affect your current position, well-being, and future.

In an unchanging form, *ATTRACTION* indicates it may be necessary to be receptive and open to all that comes into your life at this time. KEN, *tranquillity and stillness, is in the lower trigram attracting* TUI, *joy and pleasure.* A tranquil openness allows you to influence and be influenced, bringing the joy of shared experience into your life. This spontaneous mutual influence, perhaps a love affair, must be experienced before there is change.

---

* In matters of political relationships, this concept was described by
Lao Tzu in the following way:

A big state can take over a small state if it places itself below the
small state.
And the small state can take over a big state if it places itself
below the big state.
Thus some, by placing themselves below, take over others,
And some, by being naturally low, take over other states.
After all, what a big state wants is but to annex and herd others,
And what a small state wants is merely to join and serve others.
Since both big and small states get what they want,
The big state should place itself low.

TOP LINE

Words are only words. Ideas mean little unexecuted. What are you doing?

► FIFTH LINE

Look within to determine the depth of your influence on external matters. People with a profound inner resolve can accomplish much. Those with shallow roots cannot exert significant external influence.

► FOURTH LINE

The desire to influence a specific person or situation is now enhanced. Do not become calculating or manipulative in your efforts. Instead, take a unilateral approach by displaying the strength of your convictions in all that you do. By remaining consistent in all matters you will achieve your goal.

THIRD LINE

You must gain control of yourself. Don't run this way and that on impulse in an attempt to influence others or indulge in your many whims. You will ultimately be humiliated by such unconsidered actions. Set up a few inhibitions for yourself and operate within these limitations while you develop some self-control.

SECOND LINE

You may feel compelled to move, to take some kind of action, yet you really don't know what you're doing. It's a little like sleepwalking. Avoid action until you wake up to what's going on. Otherwise there is some danger of getting into trouble.

BOTTOM LINE

There is something in the air. Perhaps it's the beginning of a compelling attraction or an idea just coming to light. Whatever it is, it is of little significance, since a great deal more must be done to make it a reality.

32

HENG

ABOVE: CHEN THUNDER

BELOW: SUN WIND

UPPER: TUI LAKE

LOWER: CH'IEN HEAVEN

RULING LINES

The hexagram is balanced through the correspondence of lines 1 and 4, 2 and 5, and 3 and 6, creating CONTINUING endurance. The unusual firm line in the lower trigram of human affairs marks the ruler.

CONTINUING
(ENDURING)

Consider a flowering plant: its new leaves stretching open, reaching for the life-giving sun; its roots anchoring deep into the earth, drawing sustenance into itself. As if prompted by an invisible imperative, it forms its blossom and develops its fruit. In time its flower magically unfolds, inviting response to its sensual delights of color and scent. Nature, in turn, participates in pollinating and thereby furthering the development of the wondrous seed hidden within the fruit. Soon, after this co-operative celebration of life, the plant concentrates the total of its energies into the ripening fruit and maturing seed. In the end, as the plant declines and rests, perhaps terminating itself, the seed detaches and falls to the earth, *CONTINUING* the perpetuating mystery of existence. The Chinese say of this hexagram: "When we examine the continuance of things, the natural tendencies of heaven and earth can be seen. Herein lies the secret of eternity."

The time requires a regard for continuing traditions and enduring values. Look within for character traits that are self-perpetuating and self-renewing. New goals can be reached through relying on that which has endurance and consistency in your nature. Act out the laws of your inner Self, trust the inherent correctness of your instincts as you go about your business. In this way you will meet with success.

Social customs will offer assurances and support because of their very endurance. *CONTINUING* in traditions that are the understood bases of social interaction will now bring order, unity, and a deep sense of security to you and your community. This does not mean a blind dogmatism to arbitrary social institutions, but rather an adherence to foundations that support the growth of sound and smooth-working systems in life.

In business and political affairs, pay particular attention to the support of policies that have proved themselves useful. This is not the time to change methods of operation for the sake of change. Instead, it is a time to make these methods work with new trends in thought. Success now comes through *CONTINUING* movement toward long-standing objectives — objectives that are harmonious with a well-ordered life.

Personal relationships will now develop most comfortably within the structure of enduring social institutions such as marriage or family. The ceremonies and customs that spring from tradition will bring joy and security into your life. At the same time, your relationships should have direction and should grow and adapt to the times. *CONTINUING* traditions will create a superstructure for a flowering relationship, as a trellis for a vine. Never should they become rigid limitations.

In its static form, *CONTINUING* suggests the need to develop continuity and unity within the Self. *The lower trigram,* SUN, *with its steady, penetrating efforts, gives direction to* CHEN, *movement, above.* This direction determines all behavior and should be consistent and principled. Undisciplined movement at this time will lead you away from your goals. Listen to your inner voice. Look to enduring values.

TOP LINE

If you handle your affairs in a perpetual state of anxiety, you will soon exhaust yourself. More could be accomplished with a calm and composed demeanor. Make an attempt to comprehend and align yourself with what is truly happening before you create serious problems for yourself.

FIFTH LINE

When you are seeking earthly things, apply earthly methods. When your goals are lofty and ambitious, your methods must be inventive and daring. Learn to apply the appropriate kind of effort to achieve the effect you desire.

FOURTH LINE

Be certain that your goals are realistic. If you try to achieve things that are unlikely, no matter how vigorously, you will still accomplish absolutely nothing. Perhaps you should re-evaluate your desires.

THIRD LINE

Your reactions and moods caused by external situations are as unpredictable as these varying circumstances. This inconsistency within the Self will bring your humiliation. In turn, this creates a cycle of difficulties. Try to center yourself.

▶ SECOND LINE

Apply just enough consistent force to effect the situation. Too much energy, or too little, will create chaos. Avoid extremes in your actions.

BOTTOM LINE

Do not attempt to wholly and quickly embrace a method or system that is new to you. Life-styles cannot be changed overnight. There are no shortcuts to reform. Such things are cultivated and matured in order to bring about the desired results.

33

TUN

ABOVE: CH'IEN
HEAVEN

BELOW: KEN
MOUNTAIN

UPPER: CH'IEN
HEAVEN

LOWER: SUN
WIND

RULING LINES

The correct ruler in the fifth position of authority moves up and away from the rising inferior lines in the lower trigram of human affairs.

RETREAT

The brillance of the moon begins to diminish at the moment it reaches its fullness, while winter's coming becomes apparent even in the summer. This natural pattern of advance and decline is reflected now in human affairs. Just as life prepares its enduring retreat from the dark stillness of winter, you must prepare to *RETREAT* from a rising darkness that will work at cross purposes to your aims.

Like winter, this hostile and inferior force is in accordance with the patterns in the cosmos. To *RETREAT* at the proper moment is the best course of action. Choose this moment wisely. If you *RETREAT* too soon, you will not have time to properly prepare your return; if you wait too long, you may be trapped. Your *RETREAT* should be confident and powerful. You are not abandoning the situation, but, instead, making a wise and timely withdrawal. Until the time is right for a countermove, only small things may be accomplished successfully. Modest but firm arrangements should be made both to aid in your return and to prevent any adversaries from advancing in your absence.

It is of great importance that you do not confront or struggle with opposing forces and thereby become emotionally involved with what is, actually, a futile situation. Vengeance and hatred will cloud your judgment and prevent the necessary *RETREAT*. You cannot win the war right now, but you can stop the enemy's advance. This is done with a determined detachment: Cut off the lines of communication, become self-sufficient, withdraw intellectually and emotionally.

Difficulties and hostilities are on the rise in matters of business or politics. Do not attempt to compete with these forces. Instead, concern yourself with small internal reinforcements. The overall situation is inflexible at this time, yet a detached *RETREAT* will give you the opportunity for later advancement.

In your relationships, you may have to *RETREAT en masse* from the forces around you. If discord exists between you and your loved one, it is best to look upon it as a phase in the development of the relationship. Try to become composed and dispassionate. Your ideals cannot be met within the relationship at this time. Instead, *RETREAT* and look inward for satisfaction.

You may now be suffering from an inner conflict based upon the misalignment of your ideals and reality. If such is the case, it is time to *RETREAT* and take a longer look. Do not abandon your principles, but do withdraw from situations and attitudes that create conflict. Continuing in inner conflict will result in stress that is unhealthy for both mind and body.

The upper trigram, CH'IEN, *firmness, moves up and away from the inflexible, immovable* KEN, *in the lower position.* RETREAT *in its static form suggests that the object of your inquiry is inflexible, untenable, and formidable. You must calmly and unemotionally remove yourself from the situation.*

TOP LINE

You are sufficiently removed from the situation and able to *RETREAT* without guilt or doubt. Here you are blessed with great good fortune. You will find rewarding success in your endeavors.

► FIFTH LINE

Make your *RETREAT* friendly but firm. Do not be drawn into irrelevant discussions or considerations concerning your decision. A persevering withdrawal brings good fortune.

FOURTH LINE

If you recognize the moment for *RETREAT*, be certain that you do so with the proper attitude — that is, willingly. In this way you will adjust easily and progress in your new environment. Those who are filled with emotional turmoil during withdrawal will suffer greatly.

THIRD LINE

You've been held back from *RETREAT* and consequently are in the center of a difficult situation. Inferior persons or ideals may surround you. They can be used to insulate you from further difficulties, but you can accomplish nothing significant while fettered by inferior elements.

SECOND LINE

You lack sufficient strength to make a complete withdrawal. If you can maintain a strong desire to *RETREAT* or align yourself with one in a position to guide you, you can make your escape.

BOTTOM LINE

Your position in the situation is in close proximity to an adversary. It would have been to your advantage to *RETREAT* earlier. Do not take any action now, as it will only invite danger.

34

The fourth line in the position of social awareness gains power from the firm lines below and rules the entire hexagram.

GREAT POWER

GREAT POWER, when it befalls a man, is a true test of his character. All of his actions have significant influence upon others. What he says is heard, what he thinks is felt. He has the wherewithal to bring enlightenment and progress to his world or to lead it into chaos and evil. He can greatly further his inner development, or completely exhaust himself. Therefore the man possessing *GREAT POWER* is mostly concerned with correctness.

Keep in mind that power is a means and not an end in itself. In applying the available forces to the situation at hand, be certain that your timing is exact and that your actions are correct — that is, in the best interest for all concerned. The Chinese point out that actions that combine both correctness and *GREAT POWER* represent the true character and tendencies in heaven and on earth. The responsibility of correctness in times of *GREAT POWER* is unparalleled in importance, for actions that are inappropriate or incorrect will pull you and others into chaos.

There is little question that this hexagram is unusually auspicious in worldly matters. Although blessed with *GREAT POWER*, you would be wise to pause and be certain that your proposed objectives are honorable. Take a cue from the past. Do not do anything that is not part of established policy. Unorthodox actions can lead to downfall during powerful times. Be patient, too, and wait for the opportune moment before executing your plan.

Above all, the influence of *GREAT POWER* will be most evident in direct social situations. You will find yourself in the center of attention. Your influence is tremendous at this time; your presence does not go unnoticed. Use the power to improve relations and implement good works. When in doubt, adhere strictly to established customs and social order. In this way you will realize continued support, even after the time of *GREAT POWER* is past.

You will find that you have unusual influence and power in personal relationships. This is, definitely, a responsibility. Those you love trust you and look to you for leadership. Sensing their dependence, they may look to you for reassurance as well. Maintain now a strictly traditional role. Even innocent deviations from the traditional could end in emotional disaster.

Transcend difficulties in your inner development by remaining mindful of your shortcomings. Do not assume that your power indicates strength of character, or that it justifies all your attitudes and opinions. This is just another test. Pay special attention to timing, propriety and goodness in order to fully employ the *GREAT POWER* available to you. In bringing enlightenment and progress to others, you strengthen your own sense of health and well-being.

CH'IEN, *heavenly strength, in the lower trigram firmly establishes the path of goodness. Great movement,* CHEN, *above, carries this out.* When you receive this hexagram without change, you must devote yourself to establishing harmony between your Self and traditional ideals. Adhering to these ideals will center you, regardless of your opinions of conventional values. This is absolutely necessary in order to give your *GREAT POWER* the correct thrust — the thrust out of and beyond what may be a stifling situation.

TOP LINE

You have gone so far in the pursuit of your desires that you are at an impasse. Everything you try to do just complicates the situation even further. Seeing the difficulty of this will eventually force you to compose yourself. The entire affair can then be resolved.

FIFTH LINE

You should now let go of an opinionated or stubborn attitude. It is no longer necessary to prove anything. The situation will progress with ease; therefore you do not need to use excessive force.

▶ FOURTH LINE

When you can work toward your aim and make progress without a great show of power, you create a striking effect. Obstacles give way and your inner strength persists. Good fortune.

THIRD LINE

Only inferior people boast of their power or demonstrate it ostentatiously. This creates many unnecessary entanglements and, ultimately, danger. Do not persist in this. Concealed power, at this time, has the greatest effect.

SECOND LINE

Moderation now is the key to lasting success. Do not allow yourself to become overconfident because you meet with such little resistance in your efforts. Use your power carefully.

BOTTOM LINE

Even though you have the strength, proceeding with your plan would be a mistake. You must not force this issue because you are not in a position to do so successfully.

35

CHIN

**ABOVE: LI
FIRE**

**BELOW: K'UN
EARTH**

**UPPER: K'AN
WATER**

**LOWER: KEN
MOUNTAIN**

RULING LINES

The yielding ruler in the fifth positon of authority is receptive to suggestion from the lines below. It is surrounded by firmness in wisdom at the top and social awareness in the fourth position. Thus there is PROGRESS.

PROGRESS

This is a time of rapid progress, which begins in a particularly radiant and enlightened individual and benefits his entire society. He is, in turn, recognized and given a prominent position of continuing influence. He is thought of as an asset by both those in authority and those whom he leads.

Good ideas are now best put to use in serving others. If you are a leader and in a position to implement progressive action, you will meet with great success. You are in the midst of quickly expanding social and political interests. The influence you can now gain over others will propel you into a position of exceptional prominence. If you can maintain a virtuous and high-minded sense of social *PROGRESS*, you will be supported by your milieu, and your example will be emulated. If you are acting out of loyalty, you may now approach those in authority with confidence. Your intelligence and virtue will be quickly recognized, and you will be rewarded with advancement. Suggestions you might now make concerning the accomplishment of significant tasks will have great impact.

Communication is now of vast importance during a time of rapid *PROGRESS*. It is wise for you to stay in close touch with all levels of your social world. Monitor the needs of others and be supportive of progressive improvements. Take an active part in the affairs of society now in order to refine and enhance your inner worth.

In personal and family relationships, there is present a great opportunity for communication and mutual accord. The most rewarding aspects of family life can be seen when the members loyally support the goals of the individual and the individual's achievements bring honor and *PROGRESS* to the family. There is no room for jealousy here, and it is, indeed, inappropriate. You and your loved ones can now present a unified force socially, bringing position and power into the relationship.

By fostering altruistic motivations you make yourself radiant and influential. By developing sincere loyalties you make yourself strong in character. You can now bring even greater *PROGRESS* to your inner development by examining your relationship with your fellow man. Take note of your effect upon those in authority and your relations with your equals. If you can see a way to bring *PROGRESS* to them both, then you are on your way to an enlightened destiny.

There is clarity, LI, *in the upper realm, which springs forth from sincere devotion,* K'UN, *in the lower trigram of human affairs.* When *PROGRESS* occurs without change it reflects a sound and stable position. This lasting accord affords you a foundation from which you can improve your moral and philosophical outlook. Future endeavors can begin on a higher plane of understanding. Goals can become refined and truly worthy.

TOP LINE

Take aggressive and offensive measures only when you seek to discipline yourself. Such severe precautions will help you to avoid regretful errors. Do not, however, make the mistake of using the same force on others or you will suffer the humiliation of alienation and failure.

▶ FIFTH LINE

It is wise now to act with gentleness, reserve, and moderation regardless of the fact that you are in a position of great influence. Do not think about the gains you might make or the possible setbacks that could befall you. Continue in righteous *PROGRESS* and you will be blessed with good fortune.

FOURTH LINE

PROGRESS is coming about through questionable means or inferior persons. Although it is possible to advance this way, the truth will nevertheless come to light. This is all very risky and you may find yourself in a dangerous position.

THIRD LINE

Your *PROGRESS* is dependent upon the company and encouragement of others. The benefits of this common trust will remove any cause for remorse.

SECOND LINE

Your *PROGRESS* is not as fulfilling as it might be because you are prevented from experiencing significant communication with someone in authority. Yet, unexpected good fortune will come to you if you persevere in your efforts and remain virtuous in your principles.

BOTTOM LINE

You are restrained from advancing because others lack confidence in you. Do not try to force the situation and do not become angry. Remain calm and behave with generosity and warmth. Put your attention into perfecting your work and you will avoid regretful errors.

36

MING I

**ABOVE: K'UN
EARTH**

**BELOW: LI
FIRE**

**UPPER: CHEN
THUNDER**

**LOWER: K'AN
WATER**

RULING LINES

The ruler in the second position of self-interest is correct but misaligned with the incorrect ruler in the fifth position of authority, thus censored.

CENSORSHIP
(DARKENING OF THE LIGHT)

You are directly confronted by forces that threaten both your convictions and the attainment of your goals. Unfortunately, your position in this situation is not powerful. It will be necessary to submit to this time of personal *CENSORSHIP* and step into the background. You must conceal your feelings. Make it a point to appear externally accepting of a difficult environment. It is both useless and dangerous to expound your convictions, and by doing so, you will only invite further difficulties. However, do not lose sight of your principles for even a single moment. You know what your goals are. It is tremendously important to maintain a fierce inner awareness of them during times when they seem almost unattainable. With this attitude you can strengthen your character and thereby put yourself in a position to transcend this formidable time.

If you find it necessary, you can influence others by approaching them on a disguised level. Be very reserved. If your awareness is hidden you will not pose a threat to your adversaries. In this way you can maintain your principles, influence others in subtle ways, and stay out of trouble. The Chinese say of this hexagram: "The superior man uses his intelligence by concealing it."

It is a poor time to challenge the opinions of others in social interactions. Let things pass even though they are contrary to your beliefs or aims. You will find that those around you are not sympathetic to your vision. Hide your feelings but still maintain your inner convictions. It would be wise to react as though you were in agreement with your adversaries and yet do nothing to actively help them. Generally, keep a low profile and postpone any political aspirations.*

This is not a good time to openly examine the points of contention in your personal relationships. Your feelings and ideas are not popular issues with those close to you. At the moment there is nothing to discuss.

However, in areas of personal and spiritual development, this situation can help you learn to accept times of evil. If one attempts to aggressively deny or ignore evil, then evil is often nurtured in one form or another. Good and evil are as much a part of the cosmos as night and day. It is much easier to develop a sound character once evil is acknowledged and accepted as a part of the world.

Unless there is change, *CENSORSHIP* suggests that you may never have tremendous influence over the subject of your inquiry. *The trigram LI, clarity and light, is being totally absorbed and hidden as it moves into K'UN, receptivity and darkness.* Still, it is implied that your goals and convictions are in accord with what is best for your inner development and should not be abandoned. It is a part of your fate to be in the limited position in which you find yourself. The Chinese regard acceptance of fate as one of the great virtues.

---

* Lao Tzu, a philosopher during the sixth century B.C., states this concept in the following way:

> He does not show himself; therefore he is luminous.
> He does not define himself; therefore he is distinct.
> He does not assert himself; therefore he succeeds.
> He does not boast of his work; therefore it endures for long.
> It is precisely because he does not compete that the world cannot compete with him.

TOP LINE

The current trend is coming to an end. The bad times are consuming themselves and will become but a memory. Those who once struggled to control the situation will fall back into obscurity.

▶ FIFTH LINE

You are in an obvious and important role in this situation, yet you are not in accord with it. You are not in a position to struggle against elements that run contrary to your principles. Conceal your ideals and acquiesce outwardly to the powers that be. You will ultimately be rewarded.

FOURTH LINE

You are in a fine position to perceive the present situation with clarity. If it appears hopeless and doomed, as it well might, now is a good time to exit.

THIRD LINE

You come face to face with the perpetrator of wrong thinking. Circumstances are such that you can effortlessly seize control of the situation. Proceed carefully. It is dangerous to attempt to abolish an old and ingrained pattern all at once.

▶ SECOND LINE

Rather than disabling you, a recent injury that you have sustained on your path will serve to inspire you toward affirmative and vigorous action in the direction of the general good.

BOTTOM LINE

An attempt to rise above the obstacles in your environment will be met with hostility. If you decide to serve your personal drives and compromise the needs of society, you will be misunderstood and censured. Such is the difficulty of this position.

37

CHIA JEN

ABOVE: SUN
WIND

BELOW: LI
FIRE

UPPER: LI
FIRE

LOWER: K'AN
WATER

RULING LINES

The correct ruler in the second position of self-interest yields and corresponds to the correct firm ruler in the fifth position of authority.

FAMILY

In established families, the members adhere to their natural and comfortable roles. Their relations are based upon affection and upon a true sense of responsibility wherein the well-being of the *FAMILY* becomes as important as the pursuits of any one individual. The Chinese felt quite strongly about the value of this smallest of social units. They say of this hexagram: "Bring the family to its proper order and all social relationships will be correctly established."

When the roles between leaders and followers are understood and respected, then political situations become progressive. Leaders, like heads of families, must have inner strength and authority. They should be careful in their words and base their continuing credibility upon actions that demonstrate the soundness of their principles. Followers who defer to their leaders at this time can accomplish a great deal.

Business relationships should now be approached like *FAMILY* relationships. Such virtues as faithfulness, loyalty, and obedience can bring progress at any time, but never more so than now. Actions will speak louder than words, so don't waste time or money on rhetoric. Try to be consistent in your objectives and rely upon the guidance of authority to control the situation.

You can enrich your social relationships by adhering to roles based upon a natural affection and respect for others. Pretension, ostentation, and social climbing will work against you now. Your milieu demands enduring and consistent basic principles. You will be most successful if you fall back upon your true worth and conduct yourself with propriety. By persevering in established social customs you gain the support and loyalty of your society.

Rely upon your impulses and natural affections in personal relationships to suggest your true role. If you desire a traditional *FAMILY* relationship, then allow authority to be established and take your appropriate position. If there is a conflict of roles and your are not prepared to defer, then you may now run into severe problems. Your life will be significantly affected by the foundation provided in your *FAMILY* relationships.

Try to see all organizations, whether familial, social, or political, as *FAMILY* groups and then determine your most comfortable position within them. If you hold to this natural aspect of your character and understand the ensuing duties and responsibilities, you can more easily achieve your goals. Be certain, however, that you are not involved in carrying out a role for which you are unsuited, or a role that has been cast upon you. This will rob your life of meaning.

LI, *clarity, in the lower trigram of human affairs brings illumination to the penetrating work of* SUN *in the upper realm.* In its static form *FAMILY* implies that you are the possessor of great clarity about your role. You are, in fact, dependent upon this role for your sense of power and effectiveness in the world. As long as your behavior is consonant with this, you will have no difficulties in regard to the object of your inquiry.

TOP LINE

Your character and its development will be enhanced. Your sense of responsibility toward yourself and others brings good fortune and success. You will be recognized and respected for your insights and virtuous works.

▶ FIFTH LINE

A magnanimous and loving relationship exists between the leader and his followers. There is no reason to fear openness in these kinds of relationships. Good fortune comes through a beneficial influence.

FOURTH LINE

Attention to details pertaining to the economy of the situation brings good fortune. Any attempts to further the well-being of others in a modest and humble way will be successful.

THIRD LINE

A moderate path to establishing order in the situation must be found. A balance should be struck between careless indulgence and severe discipline. When in doubt, however, it is far better to be overly severe than to allow the situation to become lost in the chaos of indulgence.

▶ SECOND LINE

Don't succumb to impulses now. Seek nothing by force. Restrain such actions that are not part of the business at hand. Good fortune comes when the immediate needs of the *FAMILY* are met.

BOTTOM LINE

If, at the very beginning of relationships or endeavors, you establish firm roles and well-defined systems, then all will go well. Even occasions that might give rise to arguments will pass without remorse.

38

K'UEI

**ABOVE: LI
FIRE**

**BELOW: TUI
LAKE**

**UPPER: K'AN
WATER**

**LOWER: LI
FIRE**

RULING LINES

The two rulers are opposites, firm and yielding, in the centers of two opposing trigrams. Furthermore, they are in opposing places, firm in the position of yielding and vice versa. Thus this gives rise to the idea of CONTRADICTION.

CONTRADICTION
(OPPOSITION)

There is a strong sense of *CONTRADICTION* at work in the current situation. It may be a matter of opposing viewpoints — persons who are working at cross purposes to one another or an inner duality that brings indecision. You must now gain an understanding of these divergent forces and better accord yourself with the times. Great achievements are out of the question, since they cannot come about without complete co-operation and alignment. Only small endeavors and gradual influences will meet with good fortune.

In spite of the *CONTRADICTION* presented by opposing ideologies in political matters, there is a possibility for ultimate unity. In fact, the kind of unity that develops from contrasting forces is often more significant than allegiances that occur casually and without forethought. Therefore this existing polarity may very well create the ideal conditions for unanimity. Do not become impatient or reactionary. Instead, make gradual attempts to overcome political estrangement. A little diplomacy can now go a long way toward eventual order and co-operation.

Business or social strategies may appear ineffective, as they are neutralized by equal but opposing forces. Ambitious goals must wait for a more supportive atmosphere. Your best course of action now is to affirm friendly relations. Avoid being drawn into any questionable schemes. Do not make a grab for position. Use the existing polarity to emphasize the need for more co-operative conditions or for far-sighted differentiations. This will help you organize well-ordered, working systems.

The *CONTRADICTION* that exists in family life and personal relationships is classic in form. The divergent wills of siblings, for instance, are in a state of opposition. Naturally, in the larger cycle these blood ties will become the basis for union, but for the present they are opposed. There now exists an atmosphere for misunderstandings or estrangement between men and women. Their inherent polarity is at its peak as they retreat into their own individual natures. Bridging the gap that is now present is a profound moment in relationships. It is the eternal dance of the sexes, the prerequisite for significant union. Such contradictions only highlight the pleasant possibilities of exchange. Use small, gentle influences now to bring about this mutual accord.

This is a time when you may meet with the dualism in your own nature. You may appear indecisive or equivocal to others as you weigh contradicting viewpoints. Never before have you been able to see both sides so clearly. Arbitrary predispositions such as patriotism, clannishness, fixed ideas of principle or class prejudice may become less important in your life as you begin to see things in the larger overview. The struggle between good and evil, life and death, and all such opposites may appear to be simply the natural interaction of the great forces in the universe, as you develop the perspective of the sage. This sense of oneness or wholeness in a world of *CONTRADICTION* can bring you great depth of character and peace of mind.

The upper trigram, LI, *illumination, seeks clarity above, while the lower trigram,* TUI, *pleasure, finds satisfaction below.* There is a divergent viewpoint in the static form as the trigrams move apart. *CONTRADICTION* without change suggests an alienation as elements of different natures work at cross purposes to each other. You must not allow this *CONTRADICTION* to contaminate your purpose. Hold to your individuality, for this alone will lead you out of the stalemate.

TOP LINE

Misunderstandings and mistrust have caused you to lose all perspective. You see your true friends as enemies and become defensive. You will, however, see your mistakes, and the tensions will be relieved. Just when *CONTRADICTIONS* are at their worst they begin to ebb. Good fortune.

▶ FIFTH LINE

Because of a general atmosphere of *CONTRADICTION* and opposition you may fail to recognize someone who can sincerely help you. This person may reveal himself in spite of the mistrust that clouds your perspective. Working together on current plans will now bring good fortune.

FOURTH LINE

In the midst of opposition and isolation you will find someone with whom you have an inner affinity. A mutual trust can now develop and dangers can be overcome together. This co-operation can lead to significant accomplishments.

THIRD LINE

Difficulties will pile upon difficulties and you will be opposed at every turn. Although this is a bad beginning, there is a possibility of a good ending. Cling to what you know is right or align yourself with a strong helper and the matter will end well.

▶ SECOND LINE

An unexpected or accidental encounter with an important idea or person will benefit you. There is a natural attraction at work here, although a direct approach would have been inconceivable or impossible.

BOTTOM LINE

There is an estrangement present between elements that naturally belong together. Do not try to reunify the situation with force. Allow things to return to a state of accord naturally, as they will. Do not worry about it. Things will work themselves out. If something inferior is being forced upon you, a cold shoulder will work wonders.

39

CHIEN

**ABOVE: K'AN
WATER**

**BELOW: KEN
MOUNTAIN**

**UPPER: LI
FIRE**

**LOWER: K'AN
WATER**

RULING LINES

The strong line in the fifth position of authority represents for the other lines a helpful ruler.

OBSTACLES

When flowing water, the image of the *tao,* meets with an obstacle in its path, a blockage in its journey, it pauses. It increases in volume and strength, filling up in front of the obstacle and eventually spilling past it. These *OBSTACLES* do not spring suddenly in the way of the rushing water but are, in fact, inherent in the chosen path.

Such is the nature of the obstacle facing you now. It is a part of the path you have taken and must be overcome before you can continue. Do not turn and run, for there is nowhere worthwhile for you to go. Do not attempt to push ahead into the danger. If you had the strength to do so, you would not have consulted the oracle. Instead, emulate the example of water: Pause and build up your strength until the obstacle no longer represents a blockage. To increase your strength you must rely upon others. The original text states: "It is advantageous to see the great man." Bring together those who can help you, seek advice from appropriate sources, get in touch with your divine nature. If you then follow through with persistence and correctness, you will meet with remarkable progress and success.

In all worldly paths, *OBSTACLES* appear naturally throughout the course of time. In matters of power and politics, obstructions must be overcome as they arise if you are to continue on your way. The correct approach requires a certain amount of cunning, for you must either organize a following or align yourself with established leadership in order to prepare an assault. In business concerns, now is an excellent time to hire those who can help you. Or perhaps you should consider joining forces with another. Look for qualities of leadership in these people, qualities that can surmount *OBSTACLES* standing in the way of long-term objectives.

A more conscientious approach to social matters is required now. The ability to be in the right place at the right time has never been more useful. If you have the opportunity to join with others who inspire you or can help you in your endeavors, do so. Also, turn your attention inward in social situations and note those *OBSTACLES* you create for yourself.

Many of your external *OBSTACLES* are, in fact, internally generated. Whether you create them in the process of acting out internal conflicts, or instinctively choose paths fraught with certain difficulties, they must nevertheless be overcome. These struggles will take place within the Self. Often referred to as inhibitions, such *OBSTACLES* will block your progress. Yet if you focus your awareness on them and persevere in constructive and positive thoughts, you will experience great good fortune as your developing character strengthens and prepares itself.

The upper trigram, K'AN, *difficulty, blocks the progress of* KEN, *stillness, below.* KEN *meditates on the meaning of this obstacle. In its static form, the hexagram represents a situation that is blocked. And, because the* OBSTACLES *in your path do not give way, it is apparent that they are of your own making. Whatever the reason, you are blocking your own progress. Do not make the mistake of casting the blame elsewhere. Instead, use this opportunity for Self-discovery. Find out why you are doing this, why you have chosen this path. There is a reason.*

TOP LINE

Although it seems that you may ignore the turmoil around you and proceed with your own affairs, you will not be able to do so. You will inexorably be drawn into the struggle. Look to the paths of the wise for guidance in this matter. This brings good fortune to all concerned.

▶ FIFTH LINE

Even in the most desperate struggles, your spirit alone will attract helpers. This co-operation will bring you success in your endeavors. *OBSTACLES* will give way.

FOURTH LINE

In order to meet the challenge and overcome *OBSTACLES* facing you, you must rely upon someone who can help you. You will need a unified approach, employing the help of another person or an organization. A single-handed maneuver will surely fail. Hold back and unite.

THIRD LINE

If you abandon your present concerns in order to struggle with an external obstacle, you are in danger of jeopardizing the security of those close to you and, perhaps, undermining the structure of your life. It would be a good idea to return to your center and reconsider your plan.

SECOND LINE

Because you serve a larger cause, whether you realize it or not, you are obligated to meet *OBSTACLES* head on and overcome them. Even though this is not advisable in ordinary affairs, this is the proper approach for extraordinary causes. There will be no blame.

BOTTOM LINE

If you have met with an obstacle in your path, do not attempt to overcome it. Instead, pull back from the situation and wait out the trouble. You will know the right moment for action when you can move with ease.

40

HSIEH

**ABOVE: CHEN
THUNDER**

**BELOW: K'AN
WATER**

**UPPER: K'AN
WATER**

**LOWER: LI
FIRE**

RULING LINES

The ruler in the second position of self-interest is unusually strong, while the ruler in the fifth position of authority is yielding and lenient. Thus difficulties and tensions are liberated and forgiven.

LIBERATION
(DELIVERANCE)

Anxiety and strife will give way if you take firm, aggressive action now. Just as a thunderstorm releases tensions in the atmosphere, it is time to clear the air of mistakes and resentments. This should be done decisively and without hesitation in an attempt to return the situation to normal as soon as possible. The timely execution of a *LIBERATION* from difficulty is essential to success.

The solutions to annoying political problems are no longer elusive. It is within your power now to resolve issues that have blocked your progress. Deal with them expediently. When it is possible to overlook past errors and forgive transgressions, do so, for the sooner the tensions are relieved, the better for all concerned. If you should find yourself in the midst of an intolerable situation or intrigue, then perhaps the time has come to depart from the situation entirely. Whatever course you take, act quickly. Do not linger in the difficulties. A timely *LIBERATION* from the stresses that occur in matters of power will bring good fortune.

Persons and problems that have consistently stood in the way of business endeavors can now be bypassed. Many of your past difficulties should resolve themselves with ease, providing you with a profound sense of relief. Let them go and do not seek retribution. Your concern should lie in returning your affairs to their regular and intended pattern.

Your relations with others should become less rigid as tensions are relieved and a refreshing sense of *LIBERATION* replaces anxieties. You may now successfully resolve complications brought about by adverse social arrangements. This should be done without delay and with no show of emotionalism. There is no reason to dwell petulantly upon the past or glory in your newfound *LIBERATION*. Do what you must quickly and quietly, and carry on with your affairs.

Times of tension and anxiety are passing in your personal relationships as well. Take this opportunity to put the past behind you. This *LIBERATION* from emotional complications and adversity can give you a fresh new start with your loved one. You may, in fact, find the present time unusually erotic.

When *LIBERATION* is complete, when the tensions of the storm have passed, your spirit will be refreshed and stimulated. The ground will be cleared for new growth, and the future will appear promising. And, once you finally dispense with emotional ruts or resentments from former times, you will have an excellent opportunity for personal advancement. Overall, you should feel increased energy and clarity in your dealings with the outside world.

K'AN, *difficulty, in the lower trigram stimulates into activity* CHEN, *arousing movement, in the upper realm. Such a reaction brings good fortune.* When none of the lines are moving, it signals an internal process of *LIBERATION*. It may be the passing of an unhealthy habit or pattern of behavior. Perhaps you will discard a shortsighted opinion that has stifled your growth or an unrealistic obsession that consumes your energies. Whatever the nature of this internal *LIBERATION*, it is a permanent improvement in your character.

TOP LINE

Prepare yourself to forcefully dispense with a great adversary. This is done with careful planning and clever timing. This is a formidable enemy so you must be constantly alert. When you have removed this obstacle to your progress, everything that you attempt will succeed.

▶ FIFTH LINE

In order to eliminate an inferior habit or situation you must first make an inner resolve to overcome it. Only you can save yourself. Once you are liberated, inferior elements will retreat into the background and you will win the respect you deserve. Good fortune.

FOURTH LINE

There are people who attach themselves to you for reasons of their own. This is a parasitic relationship, which may become habitual. You should liberate yourself from this kind of entanglement, since it repels others who might be valuable allies in your endeavors.

THIRD LINE

You have been able to assume a somewhat powerful position, which you do not know how to control. You pretend to be something that you are not. This invites envy. If you continue in this way you will suffer humiliation at the hands of others who would usurp your position.

▶ SECOND LINE

The situation may be in the hands of inferior individuals who use unworthy methods to influence those in authority. You must now be particularly straightforward and virtuous while discrediting their efforts. Good fortune.

BOTTOM LINE

You have surmounted the difficulties in your current endeavor. The path has been cleared and progress will continue. Use this time to consolidate your position.

41

SUN

**ABOVE: KEN
MOUNTAIN**

**BELOW: TUI
LAKE**

**UPPER: K'UN
EARTH**

**LOWER: CHEN
THUNDER**

RULING LINES

▶

The hexagram is similar in form to No. 11. Yet here the lower trigram sacrifices a line which moves to the top. Thus there is DECLINE in human affairs. Because the upper trigram is enriched, the line in the fifth position of authority rules.

DECLINE
(DECREASE)

The pendulum swings once again, this time moving into a general *DECLINE*. Although the *DECLINE* points to the beginning of a later flowering, the way you handle this current decrease in resources is of great importance. This decrease is in accordance with the forces in the cosmos and therefore perfectly natural and completely unavoidable. You will ultimately benefit, however, from any sacrifices you must now make.

Accept the *DECLINE* and respond appropriately by simplifying your life. A sincere and simplified approach to life will prevent you from making serious mistakes and will improve your sense of timing. If you find the *DECLINE* unacceptable and continue the pretense of more oppulent times, you will fall into error and out of touch with reality.

Simplicity at this time is genuinely good for your inner development. You must now alter certain attitudes by curbing your instincts and passionate drives. Even in your innermost Self you must economize in accordance with the current *DECLINE* of the life force. If you normally function with a great deal of tension, it is time to modify your behavior. Become conscious of any extravagant emotional reactions. By sacrificing any indulgences that occur at the instinct level, you can now benefit the higher aspects of your nature.

This work on the Self underlies the considerations in all worldly affairs. The *DECLINE* becomes evident in diminishing social contact. Again, you should not try to force events or carry on as though nothing had changed. Instead, turn your energies within and apply them to your personal aims. Success is yours through sincere devotion and simplicity.

In business affairs, the time will manifest most sharply in terms of material loss: loss of goods or wealth. Yet success in these matters is presaged if your attitude is confident and accepting, and if you attend to the business at hand. Remember, the time of sacrifice is transitional in nature. The pendulum continues to swing.

Personal relationships may now bring less excitement and pleasure than they have in the past. There may be less meaningful communication between you and yours, and a frustrating lack of information. Don't become angry or provocative in an attempt to rekindle passions. Instead, gear the relationship down to a simpler form more appropriate to the time of *DECLINE*. Be as reassuring as possible to those dear to you while devoting your energies to the refinement of your character.

The lower trigram, TUI, *excess, is held in check by the mountainous weight of* KEN, *above.* In its static form the hexagram *DECLINE* implies that your feelings and reactions may not be in accord with the times. Regardless of the object of your inquiry, or your objectives in general, you must accept the reality of *DECLINE* and make the necessary adjustments in your attitude. Before things will change successfully, a certain economy must be reached in the intensity of your emotions.

TOP LINE

Expand your goals to encompass a more universal pursuit. In this way others will lend support. Your successes will lead you to a new public awareness. You may find this social position and responsibility a desirable new life-style and a benefit to many.

▶ FIFTH LINE

You are marked by fate. Nothing stands in the way of this. It comes about through refined inner forces that have led you into this situation. Fear nothing. Good fortune.

FOURTH LINE

If you can now locate your shortcomings and bad habits and make a serious attempt to decrease them you will be approached by friends and helpers. A humble attitude on your part will open the way to progressive interaction and joy.

THIRD LINE

The closest bonds are now possible only between two persons. Groups of three create jealousy and mistrust and will eventually splinter. Yet someone who remains alone becomes lonely and will seek a companion. It is time to strike a proper balance.

SECOND LINE

When aiding others, be certain to maintain your sense of dignity. If the nature of your task diminishes your strength or compromises your principles, or if you sacrifice your personality to please your superior, you are acting shamefully. Only efforts that do not diminish your Self are worthwhile.

BOTTOM LINE

When you are in a position to help others or to be helped yourself, be certain that moderation is exercised. To give or take too much can result in an imbalanced situation. Think this through carefully before acting.

42

I

ABOVE: SUN
WIND

BELOW: CHEN
THUNDER

UPPER: KEN
MOUNTAIN

LOWER: K'UN
EARTH

RULING LINES

The yielding ruler of the lower trigram of human affairs receives the benefits of the correct firm ruler in the position of authority in the upper trigram. Similar in structure to No. 12, the lower trigram of human affairs is increased with a firm line below.

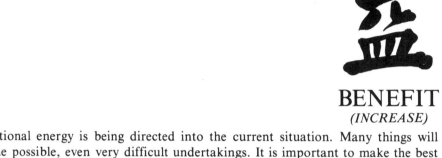

BENEFIT
(INCREASE)

Exceptional energy is being directed into the current situation. Many things will become possible, even very difficult undertakings. It is important to make the best use of your time now, as conditions will change. Pursue your goals on a daily basis and remain persevering. Keep in mind that your immediate goals should serve to *BENEFIT* your entire milieu in order to attain the successes implied in this hexagram. The kind of energy available can be utilized only on worthwhile endeavors.

If you are a leader, employer, administrator, or other figure of influence in the community, it is a very auspicious time to be generous toward your supporters. You may, in fact, be called upon to make a sacrifice from your personal resources to advance the goals of your followers. Such a gesture can now greatly *BENEFIT* society. People will be so moved by your actions that they will be irresistibly compelled to loyalty and unity, thus strengthening the commonwealth. The Chinese say of this hexagram: "To rule truly is to serve."

Those engaged in business or political affairs can use this model to *BENEFIT* their own aims, provided their goals are worthy. The time is ideal for offering especially generous services to others. This will open the way to greater areas of potential development. Generous actions, too, can enhance social, family, and personal relationships.

At this time it is possible that you are looking within, toward the development of your character. Because of the intensity of the benevolent forces surrounding you, you are presented with an excellent opportunity for self-improvement. Whether you would like to break old habits or foster new and useful disciplines, there now exists the proper alignment of forces for beneficial results. This is a particularly fortuitous time to discard a self-indulgent attitude or endeavor in order to gain a certain fundamental goodness, a sound foundation, a sense of direction and well-being. By discarding bad habits you will find you can accommodate improved and progressive patterns. Self-awareness and self-discipline are the keys to this transformation. Observe the beneficial effects of good in others and emulate these useful traits.

BENEFIT, in its static form, suggests the need for heightened sensitivity in regard to the object of your inquiry. *The lower trigram,* CHEN, *movement and growth, is increasing from the benevolent influence of* SUN, *small efforts, above.* Be prepared to assimilate advice or information about what is needed from you. A single gesture will not be enough. The situation will demand your consistent generosity. By demonstrating your willing commitment on a daily basis, you will eventually meet with success.

TOP LINE

While you seem to have the means to *BENEFIT* others, you actually do not. This is not in accord with the demands of the time. You will lose your position of influence and become open to attack. This is unfortunate indeed.

▶ FIFTH LINE

A true kindness on your part, something you did or will do without thought of your own gain, will bring you recognition.

FOURTH LINE

You have the opportunity to act as a mediator between someone in a higher position than yourself and those below you, whom you represent. If you express yourself in a reasonable manner and make *BENEFIT* to all concerned the first priority of your interests, your advice will be followed. This influential position can have far-reaching effects.

THIRD LINE

You may find that you are going to *BENEFIT* from what might be considered unfortunate circumstances. If you hold to your principles, nevertheless, you can avoid reproach.

▶ SECOND LINE

Because you are receptive to worthwhile aims and energies, you are successful in your endeavors. You may think of it as exceptionally good luck. You can maintain the momentum of this fortunate time if you preserve the normal structure of your life. Do not become rash or overly confident.

BOTTOM LINE

You are blessed with the energy to approach a large task, which at any other time you may have avoided or not even considered. Success is yours if your goal is worthwhile and can *BENEFIT* others. Consider this carefully. In this way your reputation will remain above reproach.

43

KUAI

ABOVE: TUI
LAKE

BELOW: CH'IEN
HEAVEN

UPPER: CH'IEN
HEAVEN

LOWER: CH'IEN
HEAVEN

RULING LINES

The ruler in the fifth position of authority leads the others in resolutely eclipsing the weak line in the top position of power.

RESOLUTION

The forces that may threaten you are now in a position to be eradicated. This must be done without thought of retreat, wholly in the open, and without violence. You cannot engage your adversaries in battle for, in acknowledging their strengths, you engage them and give them power. Instead, you must deny their power by making a firm, public *RESOLUTION* to grow in the direction of what is good for your welfare.

No compromise is possible. *RESOLUTION* must spring from your heart and must be voiced to your friends, family, and community. Let others know fully of your intentions to overcome obstacles. This should be done calmly, cheerfully, and with authority, thus giving you a psychological advantage such as a master of gamesmanship holds over his opponent. These struggles take place without passion, emotion, or violence but with inner truth and resolve that do not know defeat. The struggle should continue until there is nothing standing in the way of your progress.

Your relationship to society at large may require you to announce the truth openly. Open truth can lead to danger, but danger, as pointed out in hexagram No. 29, can be a very good thing for all concerned. This could refer to a legal proceeding or a pronouncement of your intentions to effect change. *RESOLUTION* calls for peaceful, nonviolent methods. Your attitude should be friendly but uncompromising. Remember, you are dealing with truth, and therefore all else must be discredited.

In personal relationships, you may now openly make a *RESOLUTION* to overcome difficulties by making progress in constructive directions. This will surely strengthen the bonds between you. When dealing with children, point out the possibilities rather than focusing on negative issues.

However, when taking a stand in righteousness be certain that you harbor no internal manifestations of the difficulties you've resolved to overcome. You cannot fight corruption with corrupt motives, injustice with self-serving interests, or lies with hidden deceptions. In the process of making a public *RESOLUTION* you must openly examine all aspects of your Self. If you are filled with self-satisfaction and pride, dispense with these attitudes in order to grow further. If you are miserly in accumulations and information, distribute them to others so that more will flow through your hands. One who is too full can develop no more and can only invite collapse.

The great power in the lower trigram, CH'IEN, *strength, stimulates and brings to fruition,* TUI, *openness and words, above.* Receiving this hexagram without change indicates that whatever your inquiry, the true struggle is within. Make a verbal *RESOLUTION* to throw out old opinions and experiment with new ideas. Only through determined, steady, open progress will change come.

TOP LINE

Danger comes from a seed of evil in your own Self, perhaps a self-delusion or conceit that blinds you. Just when you feel you may relax your resolve and continue without helpers, it will cause you to err. Misfortune.

► FIFTH LINE

When attempting to overthrow adversaries or obstacles in powerful positions, great *RESOLUTION* and determination are necessary. The roots of this opposition run wide and deep and, unless completely eradicated, it may spring back to power. A calm thoroughness will see you through.

FOURTH LINE

As you continue to push forward, you meet with one obstacle after the next. Your resoluteness has reached a degree where you cannot stop yourself. If you would submit to the difficult times and allow others to lead, your problems would resolve themselves. Such advice is meaningless, however, since you cannot be led.

THIRD LINE

Your struggle against an adversary is one you must approach alone. Although your entire milieu may be against this foe, the battle is still yours. In overcoming this difficulty, you may temporarily align yourself with it. This looks bad and you are misunderstood but you remain without error in the end.

SECOND LINE

It is best now to develop a continuous caution and inner strength. Behave as though you are constantly in danger. Through intense awareness you gain in security and need not fear difficulties.

BOTTOM LINE

Despite strong resolve, beginnings are the most difficult and dangerous of times. Be certain that you are equal to the task you have in mind. A mistake now could become an insurmountable setback. Better rethink this one.

44

KOU

**ABOVE: CH'IEN
HEAVEN**

**BELOW: SUN
WIND**

**UPPER: CH'IEN
HEAVEN**

**LOWER: CH'IEN
HEAVEN**

RULING LINES

Both firm rulers, in the second position of self-interest and fifth position of authority, encounter and restrain the single yielding line infiltrating and tempting from below.

TEMPTATION
(COMING TO MEET)

A seemingly harmless yet potentially dangerous *TEMPTATION* has entered the picture. How could such a minor element pose a threat to an ongoing situation? How can a nonessential entity seize control and create darkness and chaos in an established environment? You need only entertain and indulge this *TEMPTATION* to find out. When you give your attention to darkness, you grant it a position of power in your life. This encounter cannot be avoided, but you can prevent it from gaining in influence.

Even in a normally relaxed social environment you should now guard against the fostering of inferior ideas or persons. Make your feelings known. This may manifest most often in political affairs, for it is here that temptations pose the greatest threat. Do not give power to the people who support these ideas, regardless of the circumstances. Confront issues that seem inferior and encounter publicly persons who represent deficient ideals. Your words will have impact now.

In business matters, what you propose to do or what has been proposed to you is counterproductive. Beyond wasting your time, it could prove to be dangerous. Whether it involves a quick turnover of money or a commitment to an unproved but attractive offer, it might well create more problems than profits. Let others know how you feel in encountering this *TEMPTATION* and you will set a strong business policy in your example.

Do not expect much at this time from personal relationships, especially from persons with whom you are newly acquainted. Unavoidable confrontations may now bring to light inferior elements. The original text specifically points out, "It will not be good to marry," and refers to a person of questionable principles who is exploiting the situation. Consequences are not obvious now and foresight is at a low ebb. Openly express your convictions and desires in your relationships and you will drive away disruptive temptations.

The Self may be encountering a wholly new indulgence, again seemingly harmless. This internal *TEMPTATION* is the most difficult kind to turn away. From such indulgences you may develop a prominent and demanding character trait or a disturbing inner conflict. Exercise self-discipline and hold to routine patterns and principles. Now, more than at any other time, inferior trifles can grow into great internal influences. Casual encounters with these weaknesses should be vigorously controlled to reinforce the proper development of your character.

SUN, *penetrating work, in the lower trigram of human affairs, is interacting with the great force of* CH'IEN, *creative strength, above.* In its static form, this *TEMPTATION* may represent a dynamic interaction that finds example in the prolific coming together of positives and negatives. From such encounters, great things are born and order is established. This may represent a renaissance within, a sudden enlightenment, or an encounter of true significance in the outside world. If attitudes are correct and virtuous and no guile or cunning is involved to create imbalance, then this *TEMPTATION* may well mark the birth of a new era.

TOP LINE

Even if you withdraw from an inferior element and reject it openly, it will still be there. You will be thought proud and aloof. It would be more practical and less humiliating to retreat quietly. Nevertheless, you are not to blame for your actions.

▶ FIFTH LINE

The superior person now relies upon the correctness of his principles and the force of his character to achieve an effect. He works quietly from within. His will is consonant with the direction of the cosmos, and he attains his aim.

FOURTH LINE

Do not become so aloof that you lose contact with people of lesser importance. You may need their help and support sometime in the future. If you do not communicate with them now, they will not be able to help you later. Misfortune then follows.

THIRD LINE

Although you are tempted to fall into an inferior situation, you are held back in spite of yourself. You must now resolve this indecisive conflict. Give it a great deal of thought, gain some insight, and you can avoid mistakes.

▶ SECOND LINE

Keep the lid on the situation. Gently control the weak spots and do not allow them to show. If they become obvious to others, things may get out of hand.

BOTTOM LINE

You have the opportunity to put limits upon an inferior element and prevent the growth of its influence. Do not be tempted to allow things to develop naturally. If you ignore it, it will not go away but will, instead, become a sizable problem. Act now.

45

TS'UI

ABOVE: TUI
LAKE

BELOW: K'UN
EARTH

UPPER: SUN
WIND

LOWER: KEN
MOUNTAIN

RULING LINES

The ruler in the fourth position of social consciousness aligns itself with the ruler in the fifth position of authority, creating an ordered gathering.

ASSEMBLING

The *ASSEMBLING* of a group is the basis of this situation. The members of the group unite because of shared bonds or goals. This assemblage can be a reunion of people with a common heritage, such as a family or religious congregation, or an artificial structure such as society, business, or politics.

The major key to understanding and acting harmoniously with this time lies in the contemplation of the center. In every gathering there is a leader and/or common goal. Whether you are this leader or whether you are one of several striving for the attainment of a goal, your commitment to this assemblage is now of vast importance for both your own personal well-being and that of the group.

During the time of *ASSEMBLING* every member of the enclave must maintain unity and ensure that a sympathetic bond exists throughout. Disharmony among members and factions that form out of divergent goals will undermine the group. Strong bonds must be maintained and strengthened by adherence to appropriate moral principles, and by constant movement toward ever greater deeds.

In matters of business or group politics, you must be certain that the stated objectives strike you as honorable and that you trust your leaders. At this time you may approach those in authority with success. You must, however, have sincerity and commitment in your heart, as you may be called upon to make a sacrifice for the attainment of the general objective. If you make this sacrifice, it will bring good fortune.

Relationships may be emphasized at this time. You can now readily familiarize yourself with your position socially or within your family. Note the quality of your interactions. Self-observation within a group can speed you toward an expanded awareness. The original Chinese text points out that "by observing the way gatherings evolve, we can perceive the inner tendencies of heaven and earth and of all things."

Within the Self, too, there is a central force of character that unifies thoughts and actions. When you are not in accord with your goals, you may feel indecision, conflict, or malaise; when you are, a sense of confidence and well-being will surround you.

The trigram TUI, *joy, is being fully realized when* K'UN, *total receptivity to all men, is at the foundation.* Without change, the hexagram *ASSEMBLING* implies that your goals, your potential for growth and even your happiness are tied in some way to group consciousness, perhaps to your family or to society at large. In this position it is wise to join fully in the group's rituals and endeavors. For greatest success, locate and serve the leader, thereby strengthening the group and assuring your security.

TOP LINE

Any approach toward union will meet with rejection. This will bring you frustration because your intentions are misunderstood. Turn your attention inward instead, in order to penetrate the meaning of this disharmony. An inner accord with your Self will strengthen your position, and unity may become possible after all.

▶ FIFTH LINE

The person in this position has a great deal of power and influence within the group. Many attach themselves to him because of this. He must further prove his virtues and qualities of leadership in order to gain the true confidence of the group. In doing so he can accomplish his aims.

▶ FOURTH LINE

In this position you gather with others to serve a larger goal. Such sacrifice will meet with personal success.

THIRD LINE

A desire for unity is thwarted. The group is closed and you will feel humiliated if you continue in your attempts to penetrate it. If it is terribly important to you, you can achieve your aim by aligning yourself with an influential member of the group.

SECOND LINE

You may feel mysteriously drawn to certain people or endeavors, although this may not be what you had planned for yourself. Give in to this impulse. Larger and invisible forces are at work here, and good fortune will come by submitting to them.

BOTTOM LINE

Your hesitation to fully unite with others and make a commitment to shared goals creates indecision in your life. Only by penetrating to the center will you resolve this problem. Locate the leader or central compelling force. If you ask for help now you will receive it.

46

SHENG

**ABOVE: K'UN
EARTH**

**BELOW: SUN
WIND**

**UPPER: CHEN
THUNDER**

**LOWER: TUI
LAKE**

RULING LINES

The ruling line in the fifth position of authority is yielding and therefore receptive to the unusually firm advance in the second position of self-interest.

ADVANCEMENT
(PUSHING UPWARD)

You will experience an *ADVANCEMENT* in personal power and esteem because of a timely accord of your modest, steady actions with the tendencies of the cosmos. The coming success is tremendous in scope since the foundation it rests upon has been developed with true devotion over a reasonable period of time, and since the time is fortuitous, indeed, for the goals you have in mind. As it so appropriately states in the Bible about times like these, " . . . the lines are fallen unto me in pleasant places, yea, I have a goodly heritage."

Take full advantage of your good fortune by using this opportune time to approach those in authority. Do not be apprehensive or intimidated by this. Assertive and confident contact with those above you will meet with successful response. Furthermore, do not pause in the efforts you have made so far, for continuous activity is necessary to yield the most beneficial results in your *ADVANCEMENT*. Through the steady force of your will, your luck will remain excellent.

You may expect a promotion or *ADVANCEMENT* in political or business matters. Because of your past willingness to adapt your energies to the objective at hand, you will now gain benefits, perhaps beyond your expectations. Your superiors will be receptive to your desires, and you will achieve personal recognition.

Such recognition is indicated in social affairs as well. A gain in your social stature is coming, even though it may be unexpected. Join with others in community projects and see them through to completion. You will now instinctively choose endeavors that are harmonious with the rhythms and desires of society, and as a result you will be favorably regarded.

Rather than overshadowing or threatening your personal relationships, your *ADVANCEMENT* in influence will create a thriving emotional environment. You can now make a genuine breakthrough in communication with those dear to you. If you pursue this actively you will develop even stronger bonds.

All work on the Self is now centered in the will. Know what must be done and carry it out with unwavering effort. Through self-discipline, the foundation of a strong will can now be successfully formed. This will bring both immediate good fortune and long-lasting strength of character.

The upper trigram, K'UN, responsiveness, forms a receptive atmosphere for the fruition of SUN, small, steady efforts, below. Without changing lines, *ADVANCEMENT* will occur only with a diligent and long-term approach toward the object of your inquiry. You cannot expect to make a giant leap toward your objective through a single sweeping gesture. Instead, through modest, industrious efforts, you must build a substantial base upon which you may then reach your aim.

TOP LINE

ADVANCEMENT without constant re-evaluation and discrimination can easily become blind impulse. Such behavior will surely lead you into dangerous mistakes. Only the most careful and exacting conduct can save you from certain damage.

▶ FIFTH LINE

You are destined to reach your goals through a steady, step-by-step process. Do not let the coming heights of achievement make you heedless or heady with success. Continue in the thoroughness that led you to good fortune.

FOURTH LINE

Your progress is amplified. It is now possible for your ambitions to be fulfilled. Continue in your principles and hold to sound traditions.

THIRD LINE

You may now advance with complete ease — perhaps too much ease. This sudden lack of constraint may cause you misgivings. A little caution is a good thing now if you do not allow it to halt your progress completely.

SECOND LINE

You can achieve your aim even though you have only modest resources. Those in authority will be moved by your sincerity despite your lack of traditional criteria.

BOTTOM LINE

Although your position within the situation of your inquiry is low in stature, you have a natural accord with your superiors. *ADVANCEMENT* and promotion are possible through industrious work on your part. This will give those above you confidence in your abilities. Good fortune.

47

K'UN

ABOVE: TUI
LAKE

BELOW: K'AN
WATER

UPPER: SUN
WIND

LOWER: LI
FIRE

RULING LINES

The strong central ruler in the lower trigram of human affairs is oppressed by inferior lines above and below. The strong central ruler in the upper trigram of cosmic ideals is oppressed from above.

ADVERSITY

All physical events are natural events, subject to the laws of advancement and *ADVERSITY*. Human situations, too, follow the same physical laws. To imagine that which is man-made to be unnatural is a misunderstanding. Such misconceptions are what separate the individual from his *tao*. It is of vast importance now to maintain this connection.

ADVANCEMENT, hexagram No. 46, has progressed into *ADVERSITY*. This time of difficulty is a natural turn of events. It will present real problems, but they can be endured with the proper attitude. They may even lead exceptional persons into success. When faced with adversity, remain emotionally stable and optimistic. Hold your fears in check. If you indulge in insecurities, you will succumb to the overwhelming urge of the times and lose yourself in losing. The current *ADVERSITY* has been brought about by fate. The Chinese offer a single formula for overcoming such events: "The superior man stakes his life on following his will." Here *ADVERSITY* leads to inner strengthening, bringing success.

In all worldly matters, it will take extraordinary will to succeed. Your major difficulty at this time is that your words will not influence others. There is a possibility, in fact, that what you have to say will not be believed. To avoid enmity and confusion, rely instead upon actions. In social situations be sparing of words. Let your deeds speak for you. Your strength of character and determination will appear through your veil of silence. Thus the truth will become evident.

When making evaluations in business and political matters, keep in mind that this time has been compared by the Chinese to a forest tree growing in a tight space, unable to spread its branches. Only through sheer will and determination can this restraining *ADVERSITY* be transcended. As the tree stakes its life upon its upward reach for light, so must the superior man rely upon his will. Do not let backward trends or oppression jar your confidence and optimism. Continue in your pursuits.

Relationships may suffer from the exhausting strain of *ADVERSITY*. When two people are involved in an adverse and oppressing situation, both must be committed to the ongoing relationship in order to emerge successfully from the difficulty. Again, words have no weight here and often lead more to confusion than clarity.

Both your inner development and physical health can benefit from *ADVERSITY* if you can hold fast to your vision. Remember, if your spirit is broken, all is lost, so cast away negative or pessimistic thoughts. Since external influence is denied you, your inner development is very much the focus and major necessity of this time. The will is tempered and made strong as you struggle to overcome opposition and difficulty.

TUI, *pleasure, in the upper trigram of cosmic ideals, is moving up and out of reach of* K'AN, *difficulty, in the lower trigram of human affairs.* When no changing lines are received, the implication is that, in regard to your inquiry, you are oppressed to the point of exhaustion. Continued *ADVERSITY* is increasingly disheartening. Nothing that you can say will make a difference. There is little you can do to significantly alter the situation. Only your inner strength can help you endure. Only you can know whether it's worth it.

TOP LINE

Do not allow difficulties in the recent past to create in you attitudes about the future. If you have become cynical or opinionated, you are lost. Improve your attitude, and the situation will follow. Good fortune.

▶ FIFTH LINE

There exists a frustrating lack of information within your milieu. Bureaucracy stands in the way of progress. Those who need help are stranded. All you can do is maintain your composure until things take a promised turn for the better.

FOURTH LINE

Your progress is slowed by your position in the situation. Although your intentions are good, you are diverted from your path by temptations. There is some humiliation, but you will accomplish your aim.

THIRD LINE

You allow yourself to become oppressed by things that are not oppressive. You put your faith in things that cannot support you. You are unable to see your priorities, although they are obvious. This brings misfortune.

▶ SECOND LINE

An *ADVERSITY* facing you now comes about from boredom. Indulgences and pleasures may come too easily for you. Try giving yourself to a worthwhile cause. There is redemption in such altruistic actions.

BOTTOM LINE

You are in danger of falling into a trap created by an adverse situation. The trap is of your own making and comes about because of discouragement. Discouragement creates a pattern for failure that will continue if not halted now.

48

CHING

ABOVE: K'AN WATER

BELOW: SUN WIND

UPPER: LI FIRE

LOWER: TUI LAKE

RULING LINES

The ruler is strong in the upper trigram of cosmic ideals. It perceives and nourishes the entire hexagram.

THE SOURCE
(THE WELL)

This hexagram represents the deep, inexhaustible, divinely centered source of nourishment and meaning for humanity. Although people may journey from spiritual discipline to political discipline, explore various philosophies and scholarly pursuits, alter their awareness in myriad ways — they must always return to *THE SOURCE* of their true nature for fulfillment. The original Chinese text depicts this hexagram as *The Well.* It states: "The town may be changed, but the well cannot be changed. It cannot be increased or decreased." *THE SOURCE* contains and is born of the collective truth of humanity. It receives from the individual's experience and gives to the individual's nature. Penetrating *THE SOURCE* of humanity can be seen as the major theme in Chinese philosophy. Confucius, China's great philosopher, said, "If you set your mind on humanity, you will be free from evil." The text of the hexagram points out that if *The Well* is not penetrated fully, there will be misfortune.

THE SOURCE particularly refers to and governs the social and political systems of mankind. These organizations must be centered and planned around the predispositions of human nature. Such organic ordering then rings true in the hearts and minds of the people, as their needs and prejudices are met. It requires an exceptional personality to organize others in this way. If you are such a leader, be certain that you penetrate the true feelings of your fellow man. Without this forethought and sense of humanity in a leader, good government is impossible, and misfortune results. Social disorder and evil reign because the leader is not the right man to execute the "plan." The right man can be recognized by his ability to inspire those whom he leads. He encourages them in their individual pursuits and promotes co-operation.

In social matters, try to develop your intuition about the nature of your fellow man. If you attempt to judge others without penetrating to *THE SOURCE* of their human instincts, your observations will be shallow and lacking in perspective. Be careful, however, not to get lost in overgeneralizations or dogmatic thinking. There are countless variations on the human theme.

In your personal relationships, try to discern the biological and sociological promptings that bring you together rather than shortening your focus to the issue at hand. There are universal truths that bring certain individuals together. Uncovering *THE SOURCE* of these truths and perceiving their eternal nature will give you enlightenment, whereas a myopic viewpoint, at this time, brings misfortune.

SUN, *penetration, in the lower trigram of human affairs moves upward into the realm of* K'AN, *the profound.* Without change *THE SOURCE* indicates that it will take the co-operation of several others to achieve your aim. Do not neglect to truly investigate the aspect of human nature at work in the situation and use these insights to organize others and implement your plan.

TOP LINE

You can now share with others good, dependable advice and exceptional fulfillment. There will be supreme good fortune in your life.

▶ FIFTH LINE

You possess all the potential possible for insight and wisdom. This gift is the mark of an unparalleled leader. Such abilities and insights, however, must be applied to your daily life in order to continue growing and developing.

FOURTH LINE

The time has come to pull back and reorganize your life or re-evaluate your goals. This means that you will not be taking an active part in the affairs of others. By putting your life in order, however, you will be able to contribute more fully later on.

THIRD LINE

You may be overlooking an opportunity that has come your way or you, and your talents, may be overlooked by others. This is very unfortunate. If somehow this could be recognized, you and everyone around you would benefit.

SECOND LINE

Because you may not be using your abilities and talents in a worthwhile way, you may go unnoticed in the world. When you are not sought out and challenged by your contemporaries, your talents will dissipate. When it becomes most important, you cannot fulfill your function.

BOTTOM LINE

You rely too much upon your own opinions and perceptions and therefore have little to offer others in the way of insight or nourishment. When there is no longer an exchange with others, you are lost and forgotten.

49

KO

ABOVE: TUI
LAKE

BELOW: LI
FIRE

UPPER: CH'IEN
HEAVEN

LOWER: SUN
WIND

RULING LINES

The firm ruler in the fifth place is in a position of authority to bring about change. It corresponds with the compliant line in the second position of self-interest and holds together with the top line of wisdom.

CHANGING
(REVOLUTION)

The forces at work in the situation are in conflict, leaving the path open to change. Yet the work of bringing about such a change is as difficult as it is important. People fear change because of its unknowable effect upon the future; so when a real need for *CHANGING* makes itself felt, it is a serious matter indeed. Clarity, forethought, and great devotion are now required to achieve your purpose. If correctly handled, however, the results can lead to a progressive new era.

In order to avoid stagnation and degeneration in the current situation, a transforming change may be necessary. First, determine that this is actually the case. Study the mood of the times. Speak to others and weigh their reactions. Apprehend the needs of your milieu and make certain that this is not a passing mood, an indulgent fantasy, or inspired by selfish motivations. *CHANGING* should not be undertaken unless it is absolutely necessary. A necessary change will bring enlightenment to people and give them a working perspective into their futures.

Second, be certain to approach *CHANGING* with a correct and regulated attitude. The change should be gradual, improvement by improvement, so you may gauge the effect. Avoid haste and excessive behavior. This is not a violent revolution, it is a carefully calculated transformation. Keep an eye at all times to the bearing of the cosmic forces and be certain the proposed change is consonant with the times. It will require great perseverance to carry out this vital change, and therefore its correctness will be the major factor leading both to success and your own continuing credibility.

Finally, your timing in this matter is crucial. Because the results of a *CHANGING* situation are not evident until the change has already occurred, it is very difficult to demonstrate the reason for change. In order to gain support from others, you must carefully time your efforts. Remove discordant elements as they appear, throw out outmoded or stifling policies when they once again create problems, and establish far-reaching clarity about the future whenever the opportunity presents itself. As the constructive aspects of your activities come to light, you will gain the trust of others. Your self-image will improve, and your influence will spread.

Your personal relationships may require *CHANGING* now as well. There is some possibility here of conflicting interests or perhaps aggressive attempts to control the relationship. This occurs because of a need for a single, well-ordered vision. If things get completely out of hand, give thought to altering the entire nature of the relationship. You may be in the midst of a revolutionary change in your overall point of view. It will take time and effort to bring all the external elements of your life into accord with this new outlook, but success is definitely assured.

A struggle is occurring between the component trigrams. TUI, *satisfaction, in the upper trigram, is being invaded by the intelligent upward movement of* LI, *clarity, below.* In a static form the time of *CHANGING* suggests that although you may not know what to do, you know that something must be done. Your best course is to alert yourself by paying careful attention to the shifting moods of those around you. Take stock of the general feelings running throughout society. This may help you determine your own personal imperatives and the support you can expect in carrying them out.

TOP LINE

The major objective is reached and only details remain to be adjusted. Although you may see limitations in the new condition, you must not create disharmony by reaching for perfection. Try to find satisfaction in what is possible now and bring stability into your life.

▶ FIFTH LINE

If you look around, you will find that your actions are spontaneously supported by others. You are in the correct position to bring great change to the situation. Trust your intuition in this matter.

FOURTH LINE

A radical change is at hand. If your position is correct, your motives worthwhile and you are properly prepared, the new situation will bring great good fortune.

THIRD LINE

Do not step into change hastily, for this will bring misfortune. Yet if you hesitate or deny the possibility of change you will put yourself in danger. Rely upon openness and self-control to guide you. When the necessity of *CHANGING* has made itself perfectly clear, and when you have thoroughly contemplated its effect, you may then proceed.

SECOND LINE

You have reached a point where change is both necessary and timely. To bring this about requires a strong vision of the ultimate outcome and a thorough commitment to your project, but with the correct inner attitude, you will meet with success. You will now find additional support in others.

BOTTOM LINE

Restrain yourself. You don't really know if it is an appropriate time to act. Wait until you're sure. A little moderation will do a world of good now, whereas premature action will bring difficulties.

50

TING

ABOVE: LI
FIRE

BELOW: SUN
WIND

UPPER: TUI
LAKE

LOWER: CH'IEN
HEAVEN

RULING LINES

The yielding ruler in the fifth position of authority is receptive to the positions below and receives sanction from the powerful ruler in the position of wisdom at the top. Thus the cosmos is ordered.

COSMIC ORDER
(THE CAULDRON)

The relationship between the development of the individual and the needs of the cosmos demonstrates the meaning of *COSMIC ORDER*. When the two are in harmony, *COSMIC ORDER* exists, human potential is enhanced, and many things flourish. Such harmony can be illustrated by the beneficial relationships between a man and his superior or society and its leaders. Scholars consider this hexagram a strong indicator of harmonious accord with the cosmos.*

At this time, the decisions of leaders and politicians are wise and well regarded. In business affairs, prosperity is suggested because you satisfy the demands of your market. In general, those ideas that you currently hold most valuable are indeed worthwhile. Whatever sacrifices you must make to attain your ideals will be rewarded, and your success will confirm the worthiness of your venture, thus reinforcing your confidence. If you are an artist, your art will stimulate and inspire your audience.

Personal and familial relationships can develop into new areas of social achievement. Together you can accomplish great deeds. The powerful influence of your mutual harmony will impress your community. At the same time, you will be strengthening the bonds of your relationships.

This is a time for readjusting your individual relationship with the cosmos. There are certain areas in the life and nature of the individual that are fated, just as there are limitations in the forces of nature on earth. This is not an easy concept for Western man to accept, but an acceptance of fate can lead to great personal power. In your own life, this acceptance can bring you success in worldly matters. You will begin to perceive what is actually possible for you to achieve and not waste precious energies on the impossible, those things that are not in accord with the *COSMIC ORDER* given the circumstances of your life.

If you can harmonize your aims and desires to the needs and flow of the cosmos, significant deeds will become possible. Perhaps the contemplation of the dynamism behind the oriental martial arts will further demonstrate this principle: In the martial arts, you use the strength and force of your opponent's attack to overpower and defeat him. In worldly affairs you can plan your strategies for the attainment of ambitious goals by acting in harmony with the energy and bearing of the cosmos. Here the use of *The Book of Change* can be of great value by revealing your position in the general scheme of things.

COSMIC ORDER received without changing lines indicates that those with whom you are associated, as well as yourself, will attain success. SUN, *small efforts, present in the lower trigram of worldly affairs, is coming together and is being illuminated by* LI, *clarity, above.* The higher realms of group consciousness are being stimulated. Your entire milieu, whether it is religious, social, political, or familial, is developing in accord with the cosmos.

---

* Richard Wilhelm, in his translation of the *I Ching,* says about this hexagram:

> All that is visible must grow beyond itself, extend into the realm of the invisible. Thereby it receives true consecration and clarity and takes firm root in the cosmic order.

▶TOP LINE

There exists a general atmosphere of clarity and greatness. All circumstances are favorable. The inner self has reached a highly developed stage. Everyone will benefit.

▶FIFTH LINE

If he is humble and receptive, a person in a position of authority will make further progress in the development of his character. He will attain insights and wisdom. He should continue developing his expanding awareness.

FOURTH LINE

You do not have the capability to achieve the goals you have in mind. You have not been realistic about your position. You are lacking in either energy, commitment, information, or assistance. Going forth with your plans will invite disaster.

THIRD LINE

Your unique talents are not being used because they are not recognized. This may be due to erroneous thinking on your part. Maintain a positive attitude about yourself, and things will change for the better.

SECOND LINE

You may feel a need to stand apart from your fellow man to achieve a significant aim. Such a stance will invite envy, but this will not create a problem for you. Good fortune is indicated.

BOTTOM LINE

To attain a goal that is worthy in itself, you may need to use means that are considered unorthodox. If this goal has been a long-term objective, you may have to begin again, using entirely new methods. This is not a mistake. You can succeed no matter how inexperienced you are.

51

CHEN

**ABOVE: CHEN
THUNDER**

**BELOW: CHEN
THUNDER**

**UPPER: K'AN
WATER**

**LOWER: KEN
MOUNTAIN**

RULING LINES

▶

*The firm line in the first
position of instinctual thrust
rules the entire hexagram.*

SHOCKING

The sudden force of stored and kinetic energy in the cosmos will be released in a powerful and *SHOCKING* display. Like the awesome clap of a thunderbolt that explodes in the hushed moments before a storm, it will instill in the hearts of all who hear it an intense reverence and awareness of the overwhelming power of nature. All things in the cosmos will be aroused to movement through fear. This movement will be cautious, and cautious movement will bring success.

The time is like spring, when new growth is aroused by the forces of nature. In human affairs it can manifest as a *SHOCKING* turn of events, an unpredictable, cataclysmic occurrence inspired by invisible but irresistible forces. If your first reaction to this is fear and reverence, then good fortune will follow. A heightened experience of the forces that affect your life will bring you into close contact with the inner workings of your nature. You can examine your reactions and thereby determine how best to strengthen your character.

Once the *SHOCKING* event has passed, like the thunderbolt before the storm, the taut readiness of your awareness and caution will be released in joy. Surviving this terrifying force will give you confidence in your ability to deal with all that follows. If you can learn to react with virtuous accord and maintain your composure, success is truly yours. This composure and inner strength are the marks of true leaders, persons who can greatly benefit society. During times of shock you will have the opportunity to make new gains in social influence by handling yourself with tranquillity and poise.

This is a good time to examine your relationship to all of your external affairs. Carry on with whatever you are engaged in but be certain that you have most of the elements of your life under control. Affairs that are pending and unfinished business will cause difficulties during *SHOCKING* times. Yet if these times inspire you to make innovative changes in your life, in your relationships and in your Self, you will meet with vitality and success.

In its static form, the time of *SHOCKING* is at hand. The only thing predictable about what is coming is its *SHOCKING* unpredictability. *The double influence of the two active component trigrams,* CHEN, *movement, causes violent and repeated arousing.* Examine yourself to see if you have in your heart an acceptance of the sudden forces of the cosmos. Only with this attitude can you behave correctly. In regard to the object of your inquiry, you may experience many such shocks, which will continue until you alter your intentions completely.

TOP LINE

The times are full of *SHOCKING* occurrences which bring disorder to all of society. You cannot combat the times alone, and those affected are too confused to react appropriately. Retreat is the best course, although it may bring criticism from others who do not comprehend your actions.

FIFTH LINE

The shocks will continue and you will be faced with constant troubles and difficulties. You can survive the times if you actively change with the changes, thus remaining centered internally and externally.

FOURTH LINE

The *SHOCKING* event will reduce you to immobility. This comes about because of a befuddled mind, confused and unprepared. You cannot make any progress under the circumstances.

THIRD LINE

An external blow of fate will put to a test your inner strength. Try, at all costs, to maintain your composure. Look for an avenue of change that will alleviate the danger.

SECOND LINE

A cataclysmic upheaval can cause you great losses. Do not try to resist or fight the forces, since this is impossible. Instead, remove yourself from the dangerous situation. Become inaccessible. In time you will recoup your losses.

► BOTTOM LINE

An unexpected event may frighten you. You may see it as dangerous, and all the feelings that accompany danger will rise up in you. Yet the ordeal will end, bringing you great relief. Good fortune is indicated.

52

KEN

ABOVE: KEN MOUNTAIN

BELOW: KEN MOUNTAIN

UPPER: CHEN THUNDER

LOWER: K'AN WATER

RULING LINES

▶

None of the lines correspond. Movement stops. The ruler is at the very end and outside, in the top position of the sage.

MEDITATION
(KEEPING STILL)

There is a focus now upon your inner perspective. It is of particular importance at this time that you meditate upon the object of your inquiry. With this frame of mind you can realign yourself to the *tao*.

MEDITATION here refers to a state where your thoughts do not go beyond the situation at hand. It is not a single act but a frame of mind.* Once the mind is calm and the ego quelled, you will transcend your internal turmoil. Your inner stillness will bring enlightenment by objectifying your impressions. You can now make exceptional progress by acting in accordance with the cosmos. *MEDITATION* and inner calm will help to center you. Through objectivity, you will know when to act and when not to act. In this way you make no mistakes and suffer no consequences.

Because of the external complexities in worldly matters, it is of great importance to achieve an inner peace which will allow you to act in harmony with the times, rather than reacting with impulsiveness. Hold your thoughts to the present and attempt an unprejudiced view of the situation. Actions that spring from this attitude will be appropriate and well regarded.

Relationships can now benefit from internal stillness. By avoiding thoughts that project too far into the future, and dispelling illusions of what can or will be, you can overcome ego-generated difficulties. *MEDITATION,* as well, can prevent you from making regretful social errors.

MEDITATION, in general, can renew both mind and body. By pacifying stress that is based upon projection and fantasy, true relaxation can be attained. The instincts that spring forth will be in accordance with your real needs. Stop your thoughts now.‡

There is stillness, KEN, in the upper trigram of cosmic ideals, and stillness repeated below in the trigram of human affairs. Without change, *MEDITATION* suggests that the future, particularly in regard to the object of your inquiry, cannot be mapped out. Dwelling upon it can only be painful.

---

* Chuang Tzu, Taoist philosopher of the fourth century B.C., describes the practical application of *MEDITATION:*

> Do not be the possessor of fame. Do not be the storehouse of schemes. Do not take over the function of things. Do not be the master of knowledge. Personally realize the infinite to the highest degree and travel in the realm of which there is no sign. Exercise fully what you have received from Nature without any subjective viewpoint. In one word, be absolutely vacuous.

> The mind of the perfect man is like a mirror. It does not lean forward or backward in its response to things. It responds to things but conceals nothing of its own. Therefore it is able to deal with things without injury to its reality.

‡ Lao Tzu, in the sixth century B.C., elaborates upon the meditative mood as follows:

> He who knows does not speak.
> He who speaks does not know.
> Close the mouth.
> Shut the door of desire.
> Blunt the sharpness.
> Untie the tangles.
> Soften the light.
> Become one with the dusty world.

▶ TOP LINE

When your inner composure can reach even beyond the situation into all aspects of your life, you can penetrate the true meaning of things. From this perspective comes great good fortune.

FIFTH LINE

Once you have centered yourself, your words will be chosen more carefully, and outspoken or unthinking comments will be avoided. In this way you will no longer suffer shame or regret.

FOURTH LINE

Your frame of mind is conducive to self-mastery. You have only to transcend the impulses of your ego to achieve the ideal of *MEDITATION*.

THIRD LINE

If you attempt to force stillness upon restless desires you will only create deep inner conflict and resentment. This can be dangerous. Attempt internal composure through relaxation and *MEDITATION*.

SECOND LINE

You are swept along by your goals and the events you've set into motion. Even though you may wish to stop and reconsider, you cannot halt the flow of action. This condition brings unhappiness.

BOTTOM LINE

Because the situation is only at its beginning, you are able to see things as they are. Furthermore, your interests and motives have not yet become self-serving. Continuing in this objective attitude is necessary for advancement.

53

CHIEN

DEVELOPING

The time points to a careful and natural unfolding of events. Rapid revolutionary growth is inappropriate now, and instead, a deliberate and slow cultivation of the situation is the path to success and good fortune. Only by gradually *DEVELOPING* your relationship with the area of your concern can you make the kind of progress you desire. Calmness and adaptability along with good-natured persistence will see you through.

Although the process seems slow and at times unchallenging, the affairs of power and politics require gradual measures. A step-by-step process in *DEVELOP-ING* your position is the key to success now. In forming unions or affiliations, move slowly. Do not attempt to use agitating devices in order to gain a following. This is the time for elections rather than revolutions, for promotions and not usurpations. Leaders who hold to righteousness in their duties can now gain a prominent position. In this way an ordered and productive enviroment is created.

Your social world now offers little in the way of the *avant-garde*. Established social customs and traditional values are the keys to arousing the sentiments of others. Grand attempts to achieve a striking effect would be unwise and have little lasting value. Your time will be best spent *DEVELOPING* a position of meaningful influence through socially acceptable and co-operative efforts. In all interactions, allow things to develop naturally.

This slow *DEVELOPING* of affairs is important to keep in mind in business matters. This is not a time of quick profits or rapid advancements. Yet success does come if you hold a firm inner vision of your plans while adapting to established business policy.

When attempting to sort through the many potentials, possibilities, and problems that arise in your more personal relationships, you can find comfortable guidelines in observing established social mores. The time amplifies the idea of the traditional and the gradual. A slowly *DEVELOPING* engagement that leads to marriage was the example used in the original Chinese text of this hexagram. Refrain from hasty or passionate action and lean toward the romantic cultivation of love.

Even though you may desire to make great changes in your life, your path lies in the traditional *DEVELOPING* of events. Make an attempt to see yourself against the backdrop of enduring social values. Once you understand yourself and your duties in this larger context, you can make meaningful progress. The inner calm and sense of duty and morality that come with this perspective lend weight to the character and set a good example for others.

A tranquil and meditative attitude, KEN, *in the lower trigram, creates small but penetrating influences,* SUN, *above.* Without change, the hexagram *DEVELOPING* suggests that you are involved in a slow, organic unfolding of events in regard to the object of your inquiry. You must take a very traditional, well-trod, and usually slow path to reach your objective. This requires persistence and a constant and principled nature. There are no shortcuts in the journey ahead.

ABOVE: SUN
WIND

BELOW: KEN
MOUNTAIN

UPPER: LI
FIRE

LOWER: K'AN
WATER

RULING LINES

The rulers in the second and fifth positions are corresponding and correct in their natural places. There is an atmosphere for gradually DEVELOPING order in the hexagram.

TOP LINE

As you achieve the greatest heights in your upward climb, you become an example for others. You are emulated by those who admire you, and this in itself is the greatest praise. There is good fortune for all concerned.

▶ FIFTH LINE

As you gain an ever greater position of influence, you become more and more a target for attack. Deceitful people may slander you, or you may even be misjudged by those closest to you. Because you are isolated, nothing meaningful can be accomplished. Eventually communications will be established and good fortune will follow.

FOURTH LINE

You must remain flexible now. It may be necessary to sidestep difficulties, yield to obstacles, or retreat from danger. These, of course, are only temporary measures. The important thing is to maintain your safety now so that you can develop the conditions for later successes.

THIRD LINE

If you provoke a conflict or make a bold and forceful advance, you will place yourself and those close to you in danger. This is a foolish risk indeed. You would be much wiser to allow things to develop naturally and, instead, secure what you have.

▶ SECOND LINE

You are in a secure position. The activities that lie on the road ahead will further consolidate your development. You may feel free to share your good fortune and security with others.

BOTTOM LINE

Your position is one of the classic beginner. Criticism is now unavoidable, however — it can be used to your advantage in refining your skills. You can lay down the early foundations for later successes.

54

KUEI MEI

**ABOVE: CHEN
THUNDER**

**BELOW: TUI
LAKE**

**UPPER: K'AN
WATER**

**LOWER: LI
FIRE**

RULING LINES

The yielding line in the fifth position of authority subordinates itself to the hexagram, particularly the strong second line of self-interest.

SUBORDINATE
(THE MARRYING MAIDEN)

The balance of forces at work at this time are wholly inequitable. You are completely dependent upon a situation for reasons of circumstance, while the situation can get along quite well without you. If you try to be assertive or make yourself indispensable, you will meet with misfortune. It has never been easier for you to make mistakes, since everything you do is inappropriate. You are not in control of a single thing, with the exception of your ability to perceive your difficulties and react accordingly. It would be in your best interests, now, to behave as a *SUBORDINATE*: with propriety, passivity, and constant caution.

Your individuality is totally eclipsed by social considerations. If you *are* heard, no one pays attention. If you assert yourself, you are thought bold and presumptuous. No one is interested in your views. At best, what social contact you have is circumstantial; at worst, you are being used. Regardless, you can influence no one without being misunderstood.

If you are beginning a new job, watch carefully for early mistakes and correct them quickly and quietly. Act as a *SUBORDINATE* and you can avoid error. Do not attempt to be creative or to excel in your work or to supplant a superior. Any attempts to get ahead will end in disaster. Do only what you were hired to do; do it well and nothing more. In political matters and questions of power, it is better, now, to withdraw into the background than to give evidence of your impotence. Use your energies instead to strengthen your inner vision.

In the original Chinese text, this hexagram was called the *Marrying Maiden* and referred metaphorically to the difficulties of a nonprivileged concubine who remained *SUBORDINATE* to the recognized marriage. In your personal relationships you are not being perceived as who you truly are. You are thought of in terms of your role and how you manage to fulfill it. Your subordination to this role is an unrewarding moment in your emotional life, but it will pass. Don't force this issue with your mate, for the ensuing recriminations may be disastrous. Remain passive for now and hold to the enduring aspects of the relationship to see you through.

The time when you are forced to subordinate yourself is best spent in thought of the future. Develop and cling to a long-range ideal. This will take you beyond this difficult time, with few mistakes and increasing clarity of purpose.

The powerful upper trigram, CHEN, *arousing movement, usurps the energy and influence of* TUI, *openness, below.* When *SUBORDINATE* is received without change, it suggests that the path you have chosen, regardless of where you imagine it may lead, is actually a circle. You will end up where you began and will not transcend your current role. If you see this as unfortunate, then trace back to the beginning. This is where the situation was created and the only place where it can be changed.

TOP LINE

Are you just going through the motions? Is there content to the refined manner you present? If you are acting out of adherence to form, don't bother. Nothing will come of it.

▶ FIFTH LINE

When you can overlook your social position and stature and place yourself in the service of another, you will realize good fortune. To accomplish this you must overcome vanity, pride, and any ostentatious behavior. To *SUBORDINATE* yourself to others, regardless of their position, is now a good thing.

FOURTH LINE

You are faced with a situation in which you must now refrain from action in order to await a more propitious time. It may appear that the world is passing you by as you wait, but your reward for maintaining your principles is on its way.

THIRD LINE

To attain your desires, it will be necessary for you to compromise your Self.

SECOND LINE

The situation is disappointing. It is up to you, alone, to carry on the original vision. Such devotion and loyalty will ultimately bring progress.

BOTTOM LINE

Your position within the situation is low in stature, but you have the good fortune of being taken into the confidence of a superior. If you remain *SUBORDINATE,* you will assure your security. You can then influence the situation using tact and reserve.

55

FENG

**ABOVE: CHEN
THUNDER**

**BELOW: LI
FIRE**

**UPPER: TUI
LAKE**

**LOWER: SUN
WIND**

RULING LINES

*Although yielding, the ruler
in the fifth position benefits in greatness because the
other lines are well dis-
posed to be led. Yet since
the ruler is incorrectly posi-
tioned (yielding rather than
firm), the situation will soon
change.*

ZENITH
(ABUNDANCE)

The *ZENITH* describes the furthest expansion of greatness as in the moment of the full moon, the longest day of the year, or the heights of personal esteem. The time is one of peak abundance. Potentials are fulfilled, true goals are realized, possiblities are exhausted. Yet the *ZENITH* is usually brief. The longest day of the year lasts only one day. Tomorrow marks the beginning of decline, of contraction.

You should feel a sense of satisfaction in your dealings with the outside world. When decline approaches, the superior man does not anxiously anticipate it, for he expects such cyclic changes. He is, instead, concerned with making the best of matters at hand. With such an attitude one can easily continue as a leader. Do not waste any energy on preserving the *ZENITH* of your greatness. Do not even think about it. Your current accomplishments, your sense of justice, your present image, all that you are now creating, will sustain you through the decline.

Success and prosperity are imminent in business matters as potentials are ful-filled and objectives reach their *ZENITH.* Utilize your successes as foundations for later growth. If you feel that it's necessary, the coming decrease can be held off temporarily by expanding your objectives. By involving more personnel or resources and establishing greater goals, you can push ahead the *ZENITH* of your potential. You will, however, reach it again, since it is a natural cycle in life.

If you are investing time socially, you should find it rather rewarding as your personal esteem is in its greatest moment. You can now allow your judgments to totally determine your actions. This strict adherence to your principles will create an image that will continue to live on once your personal powers begin to ebb. In your more intimate relationships, make spontaneous affection your major concern. If you have developed together a clear understanding of what is expected from the rela-tionship, the details will take care of themselves. Then the inevitable ups and downs will be overshadowed by endurance of love.

Your motivations may begin to take on completely new directions just at the moment when you feel the greatest self-possession. Learning to understand this natural tendency in inner development is a true gift in understanding yourself and others. The *ZENITH* of inner awareness is a fascinating time for self-discovery. Move quickly, however, because it will not last long.

LI, *attachment, in the lower trigram, arouses* CHEN, *shock, in the upper.* Without changing lines, *ZENITH* gives rise to the idea of *over* abundance. It is time to be discriminating toward the profusion that surrounds you. Do not allow that which you have desired to possess you. In order to make progress you must make judgments about what is good for your development and reform or eradicate your excessive attachments.

TOP LINE

Your quest for abundance has made you proud. Your desire to maintain it has isolated you. You are out of harmony with the times and out of touch with those close to you. Therefore you have already lost your greatest possessions.

▶ FIFTH LINE

Be receptive to the opinions of others. Invite counsel from the most able helpers you know. Such modesty brings unexpected good fortune and rewarding results for all concerned.

FOURTH LINE

Although your position has been less than ideal, you will finally meet with the right elements to help you achieve your aim. Enthusiasm coupled with wise decisions lead to good fortune.

THIRD LINE

Incompetence is at its *ZENITH*. Be patient.

SECOND LINE

You lack influence in regard to the object of your interest. Obstacles not of your own making stand in the way of your progress. If you attempt to push ahead, you will invite envy and suspicion. There is a possibility of a fortunate outcome only if you are continuously sincere and truthful. Then your influence may reach.

BOTTOM LINE

Associating with someone whose goals are similar to your own will now bring you clarity and energy. It is not a mistake to continue in this close relationship until the project is complete.

56

LU

**ABOVE: LI
FIRE**

**BELOW: KEN
MOUNTAIN**

**UPPER: TUI
LAKE**

**LOWER: SUN
WIND**

RULING LINES

▶

The ruler in the fifth position is yielding to the strong lines of society in the fourth position and wisdom at the top. It is therefore an outsider to the situation.

TRAVELING

The planet is covered with communities, each with histories, traditions, customs, freedoms, and limitations. They are communities of towns and cities, communities of careers and special interests, religious and philosophical communities, or communities of racial or familial ties. They all run very deeply through time and space, and all share common experiences that bond them intricately within themselves. The person who is *TRAVELING,* the tourist of life, will touch them all but remain rooted in none. The time of *TRAVELING* is primarily a state of mind, yet it leads the traveler into very real spaces. Proper attitudes are of vast importance when moving through both time *and* space.

You are *TRAVELING* through the situation at hand. It is unlikely that you will put down roots or fashion your life around it. You are tasting, testing, sightseeing, and collecting information. Whatever the reason for the visit, you *will* move on. Because of this, long-range and significant aims cannot be accomplished. The traveler should hold to modest goals and behave with good grace and propriety. People on the move are moving targets, therefore caution and reserve should be exercised in your dealings with those you meet on the way.

In no other situation must your principles be so clearly defined and functioning than during the time of *TRAVELING.* Avoid areas of decadence and follow paths that you know are good. In this way you can steer clear of problems that you may not even recognize as such. There are fewer traditions, seniorities, positions, and rights between you and instant retribution. Therefore be helpful and humble and generally inconspicuous. Then you may experience fascinating insights without the dangerous pitfalls.

In social and personal relationships you cannot and should not make long-term commitments at this time. Be honest about your position and obliging toward the needs of others. Keep passions to a minimum. This is not the best time to eagerly express your opinions or impose your way of doing things. You should instead listen and learn.

This could be a phase in your life when you are making an inner voyage, exploring new ideas, fantasizing new experiences, perhaps a new career or role. It may be that you see mundane day-to-day situations in a strange new light. If this is not a passing mood, it could mark the beginning of an identity crisis. Whatever is up, hold to your integrity — it may become your lighthouse in the sea of the unknown.

In its static form, *TRAVELING* may indicate that you are letting the grass grow under your feet. LI, *clarity and fire, is burning a path across the mountainous, immovable lower trigram,* KEN, *seeking new fuel.* You should recognize the time to move on when you have exhausted your resources or run out of creative energies. If you delay your departure, you may extinguish your flame.

TOP LINE

By losing yourself in the drama of a new situation and by involving yourself in details that have nothing whatsoever to do with the development of your own principles, you detach yourself from the very foundation of your original aims. Misfortune.

▶ FIFTH LINE

It may be that you must establish a place for yourself in altogether new territory. Be mindful of your approach. Modesty and generosity in the beginning will be rewarded with position and acceptance. Success is indicated.

FOURTH LINE

Though you are on your way toward the attainment of your goals, you are constantly aware that you have not arrived. This state of mind leaves you feeling uneasy — knowing you must move on, and yet anxious to protect and hold intact that which you have already accomplished.

THIRD LINE

Offensive and careless behavior in your position are great mistakes. You are in danger of losing what security you have by interfering in matters that are not your concern. Those who may have once been loyal will then withdraw, leaving you in a perilous state.

SECOND LINE

With confidence and self-possession you can attract support from new environments. Think of it as the personal gravity generated by the weight of your principles. Someone is ready to help you in your endeavors.

BOTTOM LINE

Do not assume a demeaning role in the general situation. Do not pay attention to trivial matters. This is not a way to gain entry into a group or situation. Maintain a dignified attitude about yourself. Through self-abasement you will only invite ridicule.

57

SUN

ABOVE: SUN
WIND

BELOW: SUN
WIND

UPPER: LI
FIRE

LOWER: TUI
LAKE

RULING LINES

▶ *The correct and firm line in the fifth position of authority has penetrated to the center of the upper trigram of cosmic ideals. It rules through its strength and its corresponding repetition below.*

PENETRATING INFLUENCE
(THE GENTLE)

Chinese art often depicts the effects of the invisible wind as it influences the landscape. Mountains are shown eroded and sculpted into fascinating forms, trees bend and twist into exotic shapes, clouds roll dramatically across the sky, bringing life-giving rain. In contemplating the wind, the Chinese mind is inspired by the profound effect of a steady, *PENETRATING INFLUENCE,* and how this effect might manifest itself in human affairs.

You are faced with a situation that can be influenced only by gradual efforts in a consistent direction. Gentleness is the key here. Violence and radical movement would only alarm and repel. To influence effectively, you must maintain clearly defined goals over a long period of time. Your efforts should be as inconspicuous as possible. Try to imagine and emulate the gentle, unceasing wind. Success will come in a gradual way, bringing increasing clarity of purpose.

To influence a group, you must thoroughly comprehend the spirit of the community. If the group has a strong leader, hero, or ideal, then align yourself with this prime motivator. Once you begin to act and speak with the sentiments of the people in mind, you will gradually influence them. This type of *PENETRATING INFLUENCE* is not rousing and takes much time, but it makes a lasting and profound impression.

Similarly, only with gradual influence can you further develop your personal relationships. Sweeping gestures and emphatic declarations will only create distance. The time requires patience, a long-term commitment, and a vision of what you ultimately wish to accomplish. The improvement of your emotional and physical health will now come with gradual refinement.

The power of the mind through concentration is enhanced during the time of *PENETRATING INFLUENCE.* Great men accomplish significant deeds through an enduring effort in a consistent direction. When you wish to achieve an important aim, direct your thoughts along a steady, uninterrupted course. Know at all times your goal. In this way events that capture your attention will be relevant to where you are going, and all subsequent actions will lead you ever closer to your goal.

The trigram, SUN, *small, gentle effects, is doubled in* PENETRATING IN-FLUENCE. *The upper and lower realms mutually influence one another.* Without changing lines, the implication is that you must allow the object of your inquiry to influence *you.* Through a willing submission to the time and the situation, you will gain insight and perspective. You can then determine what is possible and harmonious within the current circumstances of your life.

TOP LINE

By attempting to penetrate all the myriad possibilities of the situation, you have dissipated the energy to influence. Great understanding means little without decisive action. Negativity can no longer be prevented.

▶ FIFTH LINE

If you wish to accomplish your aims and change the situation, you must continue your vigilance and influence. Although the beginning has problems, the end will bring good fortune. Yet even after the change is made, you should periodically evaluate the results.

FOURTH LINE

Energetic action will yield successful results. You will be able to satisfy all your needs if you modestly yet confidently confront your adversaries.

THIRD LINE

People who indulge too much in the deliberation of an issue, its possible outcomes and other such fantasies lose their initiative and their ability to influence. This brings humiliation.

SECOND LINE

Hidden motives, weaknesses, or prejudices are buried deeply within the situation and influence it. These must be ferreted out into the light of day and dispensed with. Once this is done, your aims can be accomplished.

BOTTOM LINE

Do not be indecisive and perplexed. If you drift about with an undisciplined attitude, nothing can be influenced. Make a decision and stick to it.

58

TUI

ABOVE: TUI LAKE

BELOW: TUI LAKE

UPPER: SUN WIND

LOWER: LI FIRE

RULING LINES

The firm rulers in the centers of human affairs and cosmic ideals have firm lines below them and yielding lines above. Therefore they are strong within and gentle without, the profile of encouragement.

ENCOURAGING
(JOY)

The time has come when you can achieve your aims through the encouragement of others. Encouragement is one of the great powers over men. It can inspire them to the heights of co-operation, even to the point of transcending the fear of death itself. When *ENCOURAGING* others, you yourself must have in your heart a firm knowledge of the uncompromised truth. Then you may show kindness and gentleness in your relations. This pleasant mood brings allegiance, co-operation, and, ultimately, success. Be cautioned, however, not to allow the situation to degenerate into uncontrolled gaiety or false optimism. The firm truth should always be at the center.

Social functions will be highlighted now. In these situations, your encouragement and kindness will win the hearts of your friends, leading the way to significant social achievements. This is not the time to be critical and opinionated. Don't be fooled by the immediate and striking effect that intimidation has over others. It wears off quickly and leaves behind only unpleasant associations. Instead, strive to create accord within your society by *ENCOURAGING* others in the pursuits of their individual goals.

If ever there were an audience for that charismatic and exceptional leader among men, it exists now. In business and political affairs, friendliness, kindness, and expansiveness toward others will create a spirit unparalleled in loyalty. Followers will take upon themselves all manner of hardship and sacrifice toward the attainment of worthwhile goals, and at the same time they will take extraordinary pleasure and pride in their work; thus the entire situation becomes beneficial for all concerned. It is necessary only that the leader have firmness and correctness within and an *ENCOURAGING* attitude toward others.

In personal relationships you have the opportunity to communicate more deeply than ever before. A strong understanding coupled with an attitude of goodwill can bring progress to your relationships. If you are involved in teaching those dear to you, an *ENCOURAGING* presentation of information will achieve a great deal. Remember your goals, however, and do not become frivolous or lose yourself in the joy of the moment.

Generally, the time of *ENCOURAGING* is best spent in discussion with others. Communications are greatly enhanced, and you now have the opportunity to enter into deep and open philosophical accord with your fellow man. You may openly examine your principles and gauge their effectiveness. Test your ideals. Explore the deepest strata of your feelings. Discuss this with others and learn what you can from them. Look for the thread of truth that extends through all things. In this way, dogma and habitual thinking fall away, and your character becomes multifaceted and refreshing.

The trigram, TUI, openness and pleasure, is repeated and shared in the realms of cosmic ideals and human affairs. The unchanging hexagram bodes a continuing success, which is dependent upon your relations with others. Keep this in mind, particularly in regard to the object of your inquiry. Your goals can come to fruition in an atmosphere of gentleness and goodwill toward others. Difficulties will arise now if your endeavors are toward the self-sufficient.

TOP LINE

You are totally given over to external conditions. Your sense of well-being springs not from within, but from what satisfaction you can find in the outside world. Because of this you are subject to the mercy of chance and the fates of others.

► FIFTH LINE

You are contemplating a relationship with an inferior element. Such a commitment is dangerous, for you will be drawn into peril. You must now be more selective in order to protect yourself.

FOURTH LINE

You are suffering from indecision based upon a choice between inferior and superior pleasures. If you recognize this and then choose the higher and more constructive form of pleasure, you will find true happiness. Above all, make your decision soon.

THIRD LINE

Total abandonment to outside pleasures and diversions is only momentarily fulfilling. These indulgences in idle distractions will surely bring misfortune. True happiness will be found in the person full of his own nature.

► SECOND LINE

By strengthening your integrity and principles, you will not be tempted by distractions that are unworthy of your attention. In this way you will become free of regret — the regret that accompanies the waste of personal resources.

BOTTOM LINE

A contented assurance about your path and principles leads to good fortune. with such an attitude, you do not need to rely upon external circumstances for your happiness.

59

HUAN

**ABOVE: SUN
WIND**

**BELOW: K'AN
WATER**

**UPPER: KEN
MOUNTAIN**

**LOWER: CHEN
THUNDER**

RULING LINES

The ruler in the fifth position is in accord with the strong line in the lower trigram of human affairs. The fourth line in the position of social concerns yields to the strong ruler.

REUNITING
(DISPERSION)

All civilizations have experienced that powerful moment in time when the separatist factions among the people dissolve into the general enthusiasm and commitment to a common cause. Although rare and extraordinary, these times are deeply significant in both the development of the civilization and the well-being of the individual. American statesman Benjamin Franklin best expressed the exceptional time of *REUNITING* when he said, "We must all hang together or assuredly we shall all hang separately."

All cultures conduct social, political, and religious rituals. They strive for spiritual togetherness in order to break up dissension and reunite the hearts and minds of the people. Take whatever steps are necessary at this time to reunite yourself with your social milieu. It is time to break up that which divides, for isolation brings discord and blocks creative energy. You must devote yourself to a cause or task of some real significance in the world, or perhaps participate in an event that brings together the members of the community. There should definitely exist an emotional atmosphere within this mutual partaking.

Those involved in creative projects should now concern themselves with communicating. Shun elitism or egotism in your work, lest you lose the true thread of creativity. Look for the symbols, rhythms, and patterns that have inspired men for all times, and incorporate them into your work. Make a sincere attempt to meet the social responsibility of the artist: *REUNITING* people with their reality. This would hold true in all worldly matters. Strive, now, to offer products and services that are functional and appealing to the widest possible audience.

This is a particularly important time in personal relationships and within the family. The family is a direct reflection of society, being the smallest social unit. A society or family that forgets where it came from cannot know where it is going. Without a periodic renewal and *REUNITING* among the members of the family, through the practice of family traditions, religious ritual or family recreation, the members drift ever farther from one another, losing touch with their roots. These relationships are the most important you will have in your life. Therefore, if you are estranged, make an effort to transcend the things that divide you from others. Focus on issues that may bring everyone together in mutual accord.

Within the Self, the time of *REUNITING* is directly connected to your spiritual development. You should now renew your inner faith, in whatever way that has meaning for you. Through Self-knowledge, reacquaint yourself with your true, heartfelt origins, and reunite your Self with your source.

The lower trigram of human affairs is held by K'AN, *the mysterious. It is penetrated by* SUN, *gentle efforts, in the upper trigram of cosmic ideals.* REUNITING *without changing lines symbolizes a consistent isolation from one's real origins. Because of this, the true nature of the object of your inquiry is not understood. You will be at odds until you penetrate this mystery. Look within for an answer; transcend your egotistical involvement, try to see the whole picture, look for the place where all things originate.*

TOP LINE

Avoidance of danger is necessary at this time, both for yourself and especially for those of your concern. This should be accomplished in whatever way possible. Depart the situation if necessary. You will not be blamed for such action.

▶ FIFTH LINE

During times of discord and disunity a great proclamation or inspiring idea is necessary to again reunify the situation. In this way, others put aside their factionalism and work together once again.

FOURTH LINE

Here you can bring dissent and discord to an end. The perspective that comes with far-reaching ideals and concerns for the general welfare will allow you to transcend partisan interests. In this way you will find extraordinary success.

THIRD LINE

The proposed task is so great and difficult that you will need to put all personal concerns aside. Working toward common goals will greatly benefit your inner strength; there is no regret in such selflessness.

SECOND LINE

Your problems originate from within. You must modify your attitudes and overcome any feelings of alienation. If you can improve your opinions and feelings toward your fellow man you will find peace of mind and avoid unnecessary suffering.

BOTTOM LINE

You can see the very beginning of discord. This is fortunate indeed, for it is far easier to reunify and overcome separation when it first arises. Good fortune.

60

CHIEH

**ABOVE: K'AN
WATER**

**BELOW: TUI
LAKE**

**UPPER: KEN
MOUNTAIN**

**LOWER: CHEN
THUNDER**

RULING LINES

The ruler in the fifth position of authority is correct in its firmness. It is surrounded by correct lines above in wisdom and below in social awareness, which it unites to limit and control the situation.

LIMITATIONS

The most ancient and basic concern of mankind is that of regulating production and consumption within the dictates of nature. Therefore *LIMITATIONS* were created to preserve civilizations. Perhaps the first book of law was the calendar. The changing seasons create time and order in the consciousness of life, which, in turn, balances itself with the limits in its environment. These *LIMITATIONS* in all of nature give meaning to life and to the individual lives of men.

Thrift is especially important now. Limit expenditures and investments, whether they are made with money, energy, or emotions. In general, it is wise to avoid any excess in behavior, from blind loyalty on one hand to apathy on the other. If you are contemplating a radical reform or an indifferent retreat, you are not in harmony with the times.

The establishment of regulations or organizations that limit extravagant practices is in order. Set *LIMITATIONS* in business interests as well. Although these restrictions can be bothersome, it is a wise plan given the current economic atmosphere. Make certain your position is consolidated should difficulties come. In this way, you and your associates will be protected during changes in the economic climate. However, do not carry the idea of limitation too far, or you may create unhappy relations. Put limits upon your *LIMITATIONS* as well.

Curb extremes in personal relationships — extremes in promises, projections and passions. Accept your loved ones for themselves, and your relationships will strengthen. If you have gone too far in restricting others, you will cause only rebelliousness and unpleasantness. Instead set limits upon the extent of your attachments.

Artists and those involved in self-expression now need *LIMITATIONS* to rise to their full creative potential. Restraints and limits are connected to personal destiny and should be explored and accepted constructively. *LIMITATIONS* bring morality to character development and significance to the expression of the Self. By setting guidelines and principles for yourself, you can successfully accomplish something of true meaning. Without limitation, you're overwhelmed by possibilities, moving from one thing to the next, never able to make a true commitment to anything. Make it a point now to discover your personal inclinations and *LIMITATIONS*, and you will discover the path to fulfillment. Be cautioned, however, not to allow your limitations to bind you, or worse, become an excuse for sedentary behavior. Use them as the natural regulations leading to health and great personal achievement.

The lower trigram of human interests, TUI, *excess, is held in check and regulated by* K'AN, *the profound and meaningful, in the upper trigram of cosmic ideals.* When *LIMITATIONS* occurs with no changing lines, it signals a situation that has yet to be defined. You must evaluate your relationship and duties toward the current impasse. The next step is to accept these *LIMITATIONS* and conduct yourself appropriately. You can take a significant step forward when your feet are on the proper path.

TOP LINE

Excessive restrictions demanded of others will eventually meet with resentment. Nothing worthwhile can be accomplished in this way. However, for your own benefit, you may require severe restraints for a time to aid in your self-development and to help you avoid regretful mistakes.

▶ FIFTH LINE

In influencing others you must become an example. When *LIMITATIONS* and restrictions are necessary, take them upon yourself first. In this way you are certain that they are acceptable while you win the praise and emulation of others. Good fortune.

FOURTH LINE

Allow your *LIMITATIONS* to become natural extensions of your behavior. Accommodate and adapt yourself to the fixed conditions in the situation. Don't carry on battles over "the principle of the thing." Deal with the matter at hand and you will meet with success.

THIRD LINE

Your extravagant behavior and lack of restraint have led you into a state of difficulty. If you are now feeling regret over this and not busy placing the blame elsewhere, you will avoid further mistakes.

SECOND LINE

Opportunity and potential are on their way. If you hesitate when the time is right, you will miss your chance entirely. Such bad timing is a result of excessive limitation.

BOTTOM LINE

Although you would like to take certain measures in the current pursuit of your aims, when you see obstacles ahead you must stop. Such *LIMITATIONS* should be recognized and accepted. Stay within the limits and collect your strength quietly.

61

CHUNG FU

ABOVE: SUN
WIND

BELOW: TUI
LAKE

UPPER: KEN
MOUNTAIN

LOWER: CHEN
THUNDER

RULING LINES

The hexagram is open in the center, suggesting an open heart. The firm line in the fifth position of authority is correct and therefore rules.

INSIGHT
(INNER TRUTH)

The time calls for achievements of consequence through the power of *INSIGHT*. To bring about *INSIGHT*, it is necessary to confidently rely upon the inner strength and correctness of your character while allowing the forces in your current situation to fully act upon you. In this way you establish direct contact so that you may comprehend these forces and gain advantage over them. This idea can be compared to the Chinese martial art *T'ai Chi Ch'uan,* where you yield to your opponent in order to receive his power and understand his direction. You then know where and when to direct a corresponding effort to overpower him. The object here is to co-ordinate your forces so that there is a minimum of conflict and a maximum of effect. Masters of this art often say: One uses four ounces to deflect one thousand pounds.

In yielding to the object of your inquiry, become totally open and unprejudiced toward its true nature. Go beyond objectivity into pure observation and acceptance. Here you've allowed your mind to be fully influenced by what you've observed and experienced. Now stop. Pull back into your character, your principles, your Self, taking with you a penetrating understanding and *INSIGHT* based upon actual experience. Think of it as embodying another's spirit, or as putting yourself in another's place. You will not lose your perspective or jeopardize your principles in this empathetic voyage. Instead you gain a valuable *INSIGHT* into something that may be, in fact, controlling a part of your life. This *INSIGHT* is a great advantage. You will know the right words to utter, the necessary yet minimal action to take, the proper attitudes to maintain in order to actually shape events.

In relationships, base your camaraderie or friendship upon higher truths than simple interactions or idle pleasures. This will create firm and lasting bonds. Generally, it is an excellent time for establishing meaningful rapport with those around you and using energies thus exchanged for achieving significant deeds. Remember that in all matters a correct and virtuous attitude is necessary to prevent a distorted *INSIGHT* brought about by guile and unreality. Once you've gained *INSIGHT* it is not necessary to take radical or violent steps to bring about harmony or justice. A few compassionate yet well-directed words can accomplish more at this time.

By developing *INSIGHT* you will ultimately create in yourself a character trait of true value, which will facilitate your dealings with all aspects of your environment. It is a natural accord with the cosmos that is enhanced at this time. With *INSIGHT* you may now lead others with true vision, or choose to live your life quietly and in good health, with little interference and remarkable richness of experience.

The upper trigram of penetrating efforts, SUN, *is enhanced and amplified by the rising lower trigram,* TUI, *openness.* Hence an open attitude achieves true penetration and *INSIGHT* into the situation. This must be accomplished before any action can take place. In its static state this hexagram suggests that the object of your inquiry cannot be affected at all, nor will it affect you, until a sincere rapport is established. Begin on this immediately.

TOP LINE

Your character has developed to a point where you can make a formalized appeal for help and allegiance in attaining ambitious aims. However, your position is not correct for such aspirations. The pursuit of these aims brings unhappiness and remorse.

▶ FIFTH LINE

This is the position of a true ruler. Such a person holds to virtuous goals and principles and emanates, to those around him, the overwhelming force of his character. Others cling to him, and there is no blame in this.

FOURTH LINE

Turn your attention to a superior person or a noble ideal and attempt to gain *INSIGHT* into this power. In responding to a larger goal, you may leave others behind. This is not a mistake.

THIRD LINE

You depend upon your external relationships to dictate your mood or to gauge your confidence in yourself. This can sometimes elevate you to the heights of joy or banish you to the depths of despair. Possibly you may enjoy such range in emotion.

SECOND LINE

Here *INSIGHT* and influence are in their finest hour. The deeds you do, the words you speak, resonate in the hearts and minds of others near and far. You may expect a fortunate and beneficial response from your environment.

BOTTOM LINE

Concentrate now upon your inner virtue. Rely upon your principles and those things you know to be true about your nature. Good fortune will come with this attitude. If you look outside of yourself for help, you may succumb to chaos and all subsequent action will be uncentered and improper.

62

HSIAO KUO

**ABOVE: CHEN
THUNDER**

**BELOW: KEN
MOUNTAIN**

**UPPER: TUI
LAKE**

**LOWER: SUN
WIND**

RULING LINES

*The hexagram is similar in
structure to hexagram No.
28 and it carries the same
sense of the extraordinary
— in this case, extraor-
dinary attention to detail.
The rulers are both centered
in the component trigrams
and both stand between the
dynamic oppositeness of the
lines surrounding them.*

CONSCIENTIOUSNESS
(PREPONDERANCE OF THE SMALL)

You must now be as conscientious as possible in your dealings with the outside world. Your sense of timing has never been more important to you. Self-control and attention to detail are the character traits that will allow you to accomplish your aims. This is not the time to ascend to the heights of your dreams. Attend to day-to-day matters and do not overlook anything.

In matters of power and politics, it is possible that you are moving into a far more responsible position than you are really suited for. Pay particular attention to the handling of your affairs. Do not let anything slip by unnoticed, and especially do not be rebellious or outspoken. This is not a time for great endeavors. Instilling in yourself a *CONSCIENTIOUSNESS* toward duties and responsibilities will bring you good fortune.

Keep a close watch over all financial interactions. Be conservative in your expenditures. If you are looking for extraordinary profits or considering daring investments, you are out of alignment with the cosmos. Do not allow yourself to be blinded by prospects of fantastic gains. Bring a little dignity and *CONSCIEN-TIOUSNESS* into your affairs with the commercial world. It is on this path that you will find success.

In your relationships with others you will find your best advantages in following established social guidelines. Any attempts at flamboyance will meet with disaster. Simple, heartfelt emotions will bring you into harmony with your milieu, whereas pretensions or ostentatious behavior will put you into a dangerous position. Social courtesy is the key that will unlock the door to success.

This may not be the most profound moment you have experienced emotionally. You may in fact find your hands full of trivial emotional concerns. Yet you will be rewarded for taking the time to ponder these delicate and sometimes dramatic feelings. Adhere to safe, pre-established roles at this time and avoid excessive displays of emotion while holding an awareness of your true feelings.

Your inner development requires some personal humility. Any manifestation of pride may lead you away from important insights. The forces now at work are not sympathetic to ambitious individual endeavors. The situation might be compared to the mythological flight of Icarus. His attempt to fly with wax wings to the height of the sun met with disfavor and disaster as his wings melted and he fell to earth. You will find good fortune if you stay low and perform your life's work with *CONSCIEN-TIOUSNESS* and personal dignity.

In its static form the hexagram *CONSCIENTIOUSNESS* reflects a constant mood of duty and simplicity in regard to the object of your inquiry. *The arousing power of* CHEN *in the upper trigram of cosmic ideals is focused upon the meditative stillness of* KEN *in the lower trigram of human affairs.* Your relationship with the situation is inexorably bound with the demands of maintenance and restraint.

TOP LINE

Your ambitions may be too great. In an aggressive attempt to reach an unrealistic goal you will meet with disaster.

▶ FIFTH LINE

Your strength is adequate to bring forth that which you desire, but your position is not appropriate. You will need help from others. Modestly seek such assistance from qualified people and you can accomplish your aim.

FOURTH LINE

Caution: Do not forge ahead toward your goals or force issues at this time. Stay low and remain inwardly persevering.

THIRD LINE

This is a warning. Because you are in the right and things have gone smoothly in the past, you may be tempted to overlook details and become overly confident. Dangers are lurking. They can be avoided with *CONSCIENTIOUSNESS*. Take precautions now.

▶ SECOND LINE

Use whatever common affiliations you have with others to bring you into a secure position. No matter what kind of connection you make, it is the connection itself that is important. Hold as closely as possible, however, to traditional methods.

BOTTOM LINE

If you are considering an extraordinary plan, forget it. The time and your position could not be more inappropriate. Your destiny lies in the ordinary or traditional, and anything beyond that would lead you into danger.

63

CHI CHI

**ABOVE: K'AN
WATER**

**BELOW: LI
FIRE**

**UPPER: LI
FIRE**

**LOWER: K'AN
WATER**

RULING LINES

The yielding ruler is correct in the lower trigram of human affairs. All lines are perfectly correct, and the hexagram can only change totally.

AFTER THE END

A state of perfect equilibrium has been reached. Everything seems to be in the best of order. The transition is complete and you are inclined to relax and become complacent. This tendency is what you may expect to experience *AFTER THE END* or climax of a phase. The situation reflects a familiar historical pattern: After a civilization's exhilarating climb to its glorious peak, decline begins; apathy and irresponsibility appear in everyday affairs, important social bonds weaken, decadence and corruption may be found in areas once thought to be above reproach.

Although the general tendency is moving toward the less than ideal, you can utilize this coming change in circumstance to develop inner-caution and fortification. Such virtues can alert you to situations that must be avoided or dispensed with quickly and firmly. Make it a point to take care of details as they arise. The successful outcome of small efforts is indicated. You cannot avoid the decline that comes *AFTER THE END,* yet you can learn to survive such times and emerge strengthened in spirit and character.

Above all, do not try to maintain the illusion of the ideal that exists now. You will be deluding only yourself, a deception that is surely dangerous. Such an attitude is not in harmony with the cosmos and will greatly confuse your timing, leaving you open and vulnerable to chaos.

Social and interpersonal relationships may develop problems. These can be endured if precautions are taken. If you know in advance that you will be faced with emotional difficulties you will not be rendered helpless by their impact. Those engaged in business or political affairs should be particularly cautioned. This is not a simple decline, as in hexagram No. 41, *DECLINE.* It is the time *AFTER THE END* of what has been a long-term tendency. Careers that are at their apex may undergo a major transition; long-established processes or products could be eclipsed. Fortify yourself with the knowledge that with forethought and preparation even absolute change can be successfully endured.

Exercise caution in your attitude toward the subject of your inquiry so as to ease your way through any coming difficulties. If anything can possibly go wrong, it will. Your vigilance and attention can arm you against misfortune.

The lower trigram, LI, *clarity, is entering the realm of* K'AN, *the profound.* You may very clearly realize what is happening *AFTER THE END,* yet without changing lines it is difficult to affect the situation. You are in the immediate center of what is forming and moving. It is much like being in the eye of a hurricane. It seems so calm, its influence and force are out of your reach. Perhaps there is solace in the thought that the less you can affect this particular situation the less it will affect you.

TOP LINE

You have initiated significant action. Do not assume that things will follow their course while you simply watch and wait. This type of attitude is both vain and perilous. You have created responsibilities for your self. Shirking them will invite grave danger.

FIFTH LINE

This is an inappropriate time for ostentatious exhibitions of personal success and grandeur. Look for true happiness in the simplicity of your life. You will achieve more by small efforts than by large displays of power.

FOURTH LINE

Elements of decay can be found in the situation of your inquiry. Watch your step.

THIRD LINE

The attainment of a highly ambitious goal is possible. It will take a long time and will leave you spent. If it is worthwhile to you, success is indicated. However, be cautioned to employ only the most qualified persons in your endeavor.

▶SECOND LINE

You are suddenly exposed, whether by your own hand or by circumstances beyond your control. Do nothing. Don't try to cover up, or attempt to make a case for your position. This time of conspicuousness will soon pass.

BOTTOM LINE

As you move forward with your plans, the pressure starts to build and you feel an urge to reconsider. You must face the fact that you will be affected by the events that you have inexorably set into motion, but not detrimentally, as you are generally correct.

64

WEI CHI

ABOVE: LI
FIRE

BELOW: K'AN
WATER

UPPER: K'AN
WATER

LOWER: LI
FIRE

RULING LINES

The ruling line in the position of authority is yielding. All lines are in logical accord (alternating) but in the wrong positions, creating receptivity to total change.

BEFORE THE END

The accomplishment of a goal is in sight. It appears that long-impending matters may be brought to fruition with an acceptable amount of effort. Increasing clarity surrounds the meaning of situations once thought to be obscure. At the time *BEFORE THE END* there is great promise for the future.

A unique and sage viewpoint is present in human affairs. Order can be brought to chaotic situations. Because you are now unusually familiar with the elements involved in the object of your inquiry, you can evaluate and arrange them in whatever way necessary to achieve your aim. It should be a relatively simple matter to bring together groups of people in social or public-minded situations. By penetrating the psyche of each individual involved, you can arrange to gratify their needs within the group mechanism and thereby gain their co-operation. Clearly, if you are considering political advancement or business investments, the vantage point of the time *BEFORE THE END* should provide you with an artful approach.

Yet, it would be a mistake to imagine that by achieving your aim you will bring matters to a close, that good judgment and order will prevail. The time *BEFORE THE END* can be compared to a lengthy trek over a high mountain. At some point, before reaching the peak, you can see in detail exactly how much farther you must travel. You will know what is involved in reaching the top because of your experience in the climb so far. However, when you do reach the peak, which has been in your sight for many long days of effort, you will have done only that. You will have acquired little information and no experience whatsoever about descending the other side. To rush up and over the top in an overly confident manner could bring disaster.

The text of *The Book of Change* warns at some length, in this hexagram, of the dangers of proceeding without caution immediately *BEFORE THE END.* You must prepare yourself with wariness and reserve. The coming situation will be strange to you in every way, unlike any that you have experienced. In the near future you will not be able to draw upon the wealth of your acquired experience, for in many ways the time will be nothing short of a rebirth.

The idea of rebirth here is a key to the meaning of the *I Ching* as a whole. The book ends with a new beginning, cycling back to the first hexagram, *CREATIVE POWER,* forever and ever into eternity.

The upper trigram, LI, clarity, is moving up and away from the lower trigram, K'AN, the profound and meaningful. If you receive this hexagram in its static form, it could suggest that you are not prepared to see clearly what must be done and take the final steps into the future. This may be a fear of the emptiness that sometimes comes after achieving a goal, or, on a more primal level, a fear of death. The anticipation of climax can only be drawn out so far before it loses its momentum and its meaning. All aspects of life and human affairs must come to an end and begin anew. The awareness and acceptance of this is the richness of the human experience. All else is an illusion as insubstantial as air. Do not become suspended in a meaningless midbreath.

TOP LINE

After the struggles are over there is a prevailing sense of well being which comes from the promise of a refreshing new time. Enjoy this time of celebration but do not indulge in excess, or your vision and, therefore, your confidence may be lost.

▶ FIFTH LINE

Honest determination and correct principles have banished difficulties and created the stimulating environment of an advanced society. A superior personality can now rally others around him and lead them into a bright new era. Great things can be attained.

FOURTH LINE

There is an unavoidable struggle at hand, perhaps a battle of principles. Develop discipline and determination, for the battle must be fought without misgiving to its end. Rewards will come later. Good fortune.

THIRD LINE

The continuing pursuit of your aim will bring you frustration because it cannot be achieved within your current situation. If you must achieve this particular goal, it would be better to begin anew, with the aid of new friends. Otherwise you may dull your energies and vision with discouragement.

SECOND LINE

Even though you may know what must be done, the time is not right for action. Exercise patience and develop strength. If you maintain an inner determination to proceed when the opportunity presents itself, you will be successful. Do not allow this delay to turn you away from your goal.

BOTTOM LINE

There is a strong urge to end a chaotic situation, yet it is not the time for clearheaded action. You do not see clearly all of the implications and consequences of your actions. Any actions will bring you problems and, perhaps, disgrace.

Chinese Pronunciation

In the Western world the most widespread system of pronunciation of Romanized Chinese words is the Wade System. The vowels and consonants differ greatly from English. For example, *I Ching* is pronounce "yee jing" and *tao* is pronounced "dow." The trigram names are pronounced as follows:

Ch'ien	(Chēē ĕn)
Tui	(Dway)
Li	(Lēē)
Chen	(Jen)
Sun	(Soon)
K'an	(Cŭn)
Ken	(Gen)
K'un	(Kwen)

In general, the Wade System summarizes the pronunciation of Chinese words as follows:

ai = *y*
ao = *ow* as in *how*
an = *ān*
ang = *ong*
eh = *j*
ch' = *ch*
e = *ŭ*
eh = *e* as in *get*
ei = *ā*
en = *en* as in *men*
hs = *s* as in *south*
hua = *hwa*
huo = *hwo*
hui = *whey*
i = *ēē*
j = *r*
k = *g*
k' = *k*
p = *b*
p' = *p*
t = *d*
t' = *t*
ts = *ds*
ts' = *ts*
tz = *dz*
tz' = *tz*
u = *oo* as in *too*

The Fu Hsi and King Wen Arrangements

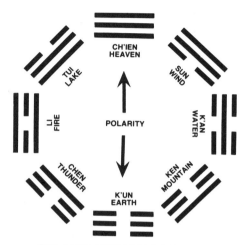

FU HSI ARRANGEMENT

The original arrangement of the trigrams is attributed to Fu Hsi. It is most often referred to as the World of Thought or Ideas and represents the dynamic reaction of opposites, a fixed condition of the universe. Examples of both of these diagrams are often found in early Chinese art.

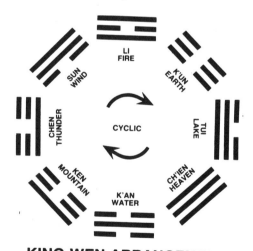

KING WEN ARRANGEMENT

The King Wen arrangement of the trigrams is something of a mystery to scholars. Also referred to as the World of Phenomena or Senses, it is said to represent the cycle of growth and decay in nature. Some scholars maintain that this arrangement can be deciphered only by higher beings and refers specifically to the external manifestation of divine thought.

The King Wen
Sequence of Hexagrams

The following arrangement of the sixty-four hexagrams is the oldest known and represents the sequence in which they appear in *The Book of Change*. Each odd numbered hexagram is followed by a hexagram that is either its opposite or its inverse (that is, stood on its head). There is some mystery surrounding the sequence of the odd numbered hexagrams. Scholars and mathematicians are unable to unlock the code which generates the order of these odd hexagrams. Perhaps the logic of their arrangement is approachable only on the intuitive level, that is, by considering the order of the hexagrams in terms of the human affairs they represent.

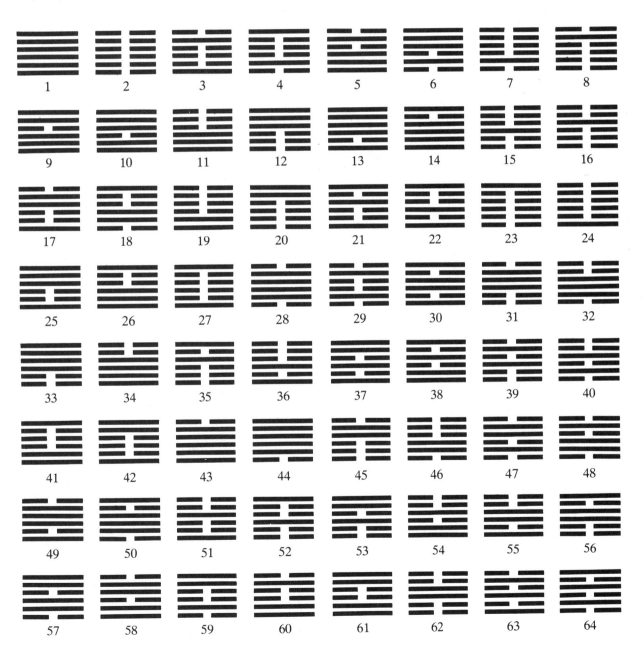

Hexagram Journal

UPPER TRIGRAM ▷ / LOWER TRIGRAM ▽	CH'IEN	CHEN	K'AN	KEN	K'UN	SUN	LI	TUI
CH'IEN	1	34	5	26	11	9	14	43
CHEN	25	51	3	27	24	42	21	17
K'AN	6	40	29	4	7	59	64	47
KEN	33	62	39	52	15	53	56	31
K'UN	12	16	8	23	2	20	35	45
SUN	44	32	48	18	46	57	50	28
LI	13	55	63	22	36	37	30	49
TUI	10	54	60	41	19	61	38	58